Louise Baron-Kent

without providence

A Child in the Hands
of an Abusive Father

TATE PUBLISHING & *Enterprises*

The opinions expressed by the author are not necessarily those of Tate Publishing, LLC.

Published by Tate Publishing & Enterprises, LLC
127 E. Trade Center Terrace | Mustang, Oklahoma 73064 USA
1.888.361.9473 | www.tatepublishing.com

Tate Publishing is committed to excellence in the publishing industry. The company reflects the philosophy established by the founders, based on Psalm 68:11,
"The Lord gave the word and great was the company of those who published it."

Published in the United States of America
ISBN: 978-1-61777-295-5
1. Biography & Autobiography; Personal Memoirs
2. Social Science; Sociology, Marriage & Family
11.03.16

This book was written especially for and is dedicated to my precious grandson. I love you with all of my heart.

Acknowledgments

A special thank you to my sister and friend, Chris, for her participation and time she devoted with proofing and editing my work in progress. A special thank you to my wonderful friend, JB, for her time in helping with proofing and revising. But most of all, a very special thank you to my husband and best friend, Wally, for keeping peace in the household, which allowed me to work uninterrupted.

Table of Contents

Introduction

Because the story that is being shared with the world here, in this book, is an absolutely true story about the evils that invaded our family, and because it involves the life of a very young child, it was necessary for the protection of that child to change the names of all participants and the place where the story unfolds. The subject matter is about domestic violence and domestic violence by proxy, which is prevalent throughout the world, so any similarities of circumstance to other situations are coincidental and unrelated to this writing.

This book has been written as a testimonial for my grandson. In the event that he should, for some reason beyond our control, once again be removed from his mother's care and our involvement with her in his care, it was written so that he would know someday what happened to his mother at the hands of his father and his father's family. It has been written so that he will know why his mother and his maternal grandparents were sometimes absent from his life. There was no way for us to prevent the actions of others and the courts. It was not because he did anything wrong, and it was not because I or my family stopped loving him. My family never stopped loving him, and thoughts of him consumed every waking moment of every day, and I have worked very hard to bring him back into the lives of my family. It is about truth and honor that I speak of here.

It is important for me to bare my soul and tell most of the evils that have happened to my family. By writing this book, I have committed the ugliness of this story to print. It has been cathartic for me, and now it is time for me to let it all go and begin the healing process and strengthen the bonds between a mother, the grandparents, and a wonderful child.

This book has been written for anyone who has ever been the victim of domestic violence or has suffered any type of abuse at the hands of another person. It has been written for those who have experienced an acrimonious divorce firsthand and can identify with all of the pain and heartache of such an event. This information needs to be shared with others so that perhaps someone may benefit from the tragedy of another, and if others have already experienced what my family has managed to survive, my family's situation needs to be brought out into the open so that others will know that they are not alone.

In the Beginning

2005

Slowly closing my eyes and allowing my mind to drift, unrestricted, I could still feel the pangs of joy and exhilaration surging through my flesh as I remembered the day my daughter told me that she and her husband were going to have a baby. It was shortly after they returned from their honeymoon. Excitement was truly an understatement of what I was feeling. Melinda could not wait to have children of her own to love and to nurture. It was so hard to imagine that my baby was finally going to have a baby of her own. We were both so happy, and I loved this unborn child from that moment! I began planning all of the things that we would be able to do together.

I had a whole collection of books on witches, goblins, and sorcerers that I envisioned reading to the child on a winter's afternoon, cuddled up on the daybed in the den, sipping hot chocolate, and munching on homemade cookies that we baked together, when the child was old enough. And I hoped that my grandchild would share in my passion for jewelry, and I would finally have somebody to leave all of my treasures to when I passed on. It never occurred to me that the child soon to be born to my family would be a boy. Oh, silly me! Filled with wonderment and hope, anxiety was my constant companion as I awaited this very special birth day.

The thought of a new little life in our home transported me way back in time to the wonderful memories of the day when Melinda was born, some thirty-five years earlier.

When I married, I decided that I would have six children—all boys! What on earth was I thinking? God was good and blessed me with only one precious little boy, some six years prior to blessing me with a second child, Melinda. From the moment I found out that I was in the family way, I prayed constantly: *Please let this baby be a girl.* I wanted a child who was sweet and feminine. Someone who could share in all the things that I enjoyed: dressing up; big, bold jewelry; exotic hairdos; idle gossip, the girly things that females do.

Melinda was due at the end of September, but, just like her own child, she did not want to make her entrance into this world. She steadfastly held on until the thirty-first day of October, Halloween. It was a day that she always would associate with her birth. That's how special she was, or so she thought. She entered the world very quickly on that day, no wasting any time. I was already in the hospital, awaiting inducement, when I awoke at five a.m. and found that I was sitting in a puddle of water. *Oops!* I thought, *I must have wet my pants.* "No, no, no," the nurse advised.

The water had broken, and it would not be long now. Around eight a.m. I was in so much pain that even I could confirm that I was in labor. I became very vocal in requesting pain medication. But it was too late. It took a total of fifty-five minutes from the first pain to her birth, all with no pain medication—*ouch*! She came out hooting and hollering, and she never stopped. She always did things in her own way and on her own sweet time.

She was so angelic looking but oh, so very opinionated. She always knew exactly what she wanted and was not about to settle for anything less. She grew to be a caring and compassionate child. Loyal to her friends and family, always involved in the community and befriending the elderly and the downtrodden, her goals for life were recognized from an early age. She was always participating in extracurricular activities. To her, it was not about being the absolute number one in everything she did, but rather, it was important for her to participate in life and do her part in making this a better world. She loved children, and she loved animals, and she loved anyone who needed help. School was not exactly her strong point, but as long as she gave it her best effort, that's what was important to us. She was an absolute delight to her grandmother, who always arrived at least one hour early in order to save the best seats available for cheering at every school event. She never missed a beat for her beloved grandchild.

Melinda went to high school at a private boarding school in the mountains of New Hampshire, where an outdoor winter activity of her choosing was on the curriculum each year. It was a place where family was always welcome and family values were of the highest importance. It was a place where God, country, and others were all intertwined and interrelated in to the actualization of self. It was communal living at its very best. Everyone was involved in the day-to-day operation of the school from the headmaster all the way down to the hired help cleaning and cooking, in addition to all of the visitors. There was participation for all. There was interaction at every level with anyone involved in any activities at the school on a daily basis. It was a Waldorf school, where the emphasis was placed on collectivism and community rather than on competing and high scoring or besting anyone for anything. She participated wholeheartedly, and she flourished.

In her senior year of high school, Melinda was chosen from among all the seniors to attend a Waldorf School in London, England, as an exchange student. She was fifteen years old, and, although there was not a language barrier involved in this exchange, there certainly was tremendous culture shock. It turned out to be an experience of a lifetime. She learned to be responsible, and she learned how to be resourceful.

As she matured and grew from her life experiences thus far, she understood the importance of helping people and taking care of the environment. She was far ahead of the rest of society in her global thinking. Honesty and integrity were her two most cherished virtues. She had a good head for being able to handle money and to plan and prepare for whatever life presented, and it served her well throughout her life.

I was very proud of Melinda and all that she had accomplished. She was an educated woman, and she was a good person, a caring person, and a compassionate individual. Her mission in life was to help fix people who needed help, and in so doing, she unknowingly put herself at risk.

She moved out of the security of our home the minute she turned eighteen. Apparently she thought that age was the magic number to prove one's independence. However, her independence and the life's lessons from that experience were not as pleasant as she had envisioned. Shortly thereafter, she moved back home. Perhaps she looked at independence and responsibility differently, and the world was showing her something other than what her expectations were. So off came those rose-colored glasses, and reality quickly took hold.

Our home was a place of safety and unconditional love, a place to revitalize, rethink, and re-evaluate choices and make important life decisions. College was a given for her, and when she finished her undergraduate education, she worked hard in evolving into that responsible, truthful, independent person presented in early womanhood. She had a good amount of boyfriends, most of whom we liked, but she wanted that perfect someone. She wanted to wait for that person who could truly be a partner in life, to have a person with whom she could have a house, some children, and lots of love for all. It was important for her to be established in her employment and to be leading a productive life before she could settle down. She wanted to be secure and to not have to worry about mundane things. She lived on her own in her own apartment on and off through the years and eventually moved into an apartment that was right next door to us above our garage. That suited her perfectly, as she was close enough to her parents but not living with them. It was an ideal situation for all. Melinda had always been headstrong and knew exactly how she wanted her life to play out. She would not settle for something that was not exactly right for her.

When Melinda and Stefan first met, we also fell in love with him. His quiet demeanor and portrayed innocence really made us feel confident that he was the perfect man for our daughter to marry and have children with. They had so much in common and shared a passion for participating in daredevil activities, like skydiving and scuba. Michael, my husband, and I thought that the two of them could conquer the world. They both had so much to offer, and we were all full of promise and hope.

They met in the summer of 2004 and fell quickly in love and planned to marry. We thought this was moving rather too quickly, and we wanted them to take their time to get to know each other. But they were both thirty-five years old, and Melinda's biological clock was ticking. If she had any hope of having a healthy baby, she had better get a move on.

So we began the process of courtship, the family affair, the getting-to-know-everyone phase of the relationship. On a blustery afternoon one fall Sunday, his mother, Erin, and stepfather, Jim came to our boat to visit and to meet us for the first time. There was great anticipation and trepidation in meeting the "in-laws" for the first time, but excitement abounded. His mother baked a nice cake for our first meeting, and we sat around on the back deck, eating cake and drinking coffee, getting to know each other. Small talk soon erupted into more serious conversation about the young couple, about the situation at hand, and about other family members and the like.

I couldn't help giving both of them a serious looking over in an attempt to size them up and see if I could discover what they were all about. Erin was a woman of short stature and very pleasing to the eye. She wasn't thin, but she wasn't obese either. Her complexion was nice and not overly made up. Her hair was blonde and worn in a short bob. She was well dressed for visiting on a boat, but she had an air of sophistication about her.

The one problem that bothered me about her was that she was always smiling. This made me really untrusting of her, and when this smiling continued even when we talked about serious topics, it became an issue for me. She continued to sit there and look at us, and the smile never left her face. It made me very uncomfortable to look her in the eye. Inwardly I scolded myself and told myself to be charitable; after all, perhaps the poor woman had some physical facial impediment.

He on the other hand was somewhat taller than his wife, casually dressed but quite plump. They appeared to be a fun-loving couple, and I was anxious to learn more about them. "So, how long have you and Jim been married?" I asked Erin.

And she, with her never ending smile said, "I've been married four times. I've only been married to Jim for a couple of years." She proceeded to recount all information associated to all of her other marriages, and he puffed up and boasted, "I left my wife of thirty-eight years to marry Erin." Erin was still smiling as Jim continued to brag how their relationship developed.

"Erin and I both worked for the same company, and we were both on the same company bowling team. We made it a point to stop every bowling night and get a bite to eat together at some out-of-the-way restaurant and share a bottle of wine so we could relax after an exhausting day of work and then a real physical challenge in an evening of bowling. Before long bowling night became a night that we could just be together, and one bottle of wine turned into several bottles of wine that we would share. We discovered that we were very compatible people and made it our goal to be together."

He could have knocked me off of my chair with a feather. I wasn't expecting such detailed information at a first meeting.

I remember thinking to myself and grappling for an adequate answer to "what kind of a man leaves his wife of thirty-eight years?"

I looked at them both and could clearly see that she was a few years younger than he, and she was quite attractive but had that very plastic and phony smile. At that moment it was easy to see, on his part anyway, that the relationship was definitely a "mid-life crisis" of some sort and purely sexual. My heart sank into uneasiness, and sadness overcame me for the family he had left behind in order to satisfy his own physical needs.

Things were now becoming abundantly clear and perhaps even bordered on the possibility of being way too much information for a first meeting. We had planned a cookout on the back of our boat, but the weather did not cooperate. It was very windy and not safe for such an event. We all ended up going to Marty's Restaurant for lobsters.

For Thanksgiving that year, we were all invited to Erin and Jim's house for dinner. I sent flowers for the table to show my appreciation for being invited to their house on such an important day. The only other outsiders at the dinner were Stan and Gwen, their friends from the neighborhood at an earlier time. I also brought along some of my famous apple crisp. It was better than any I've had in any restaurant, and it was my own secret recipe. Stefan's mother was furious that I brought this dessert. I could not imagine what I had done wrong. In fact, it would have been quite impolite to not bring something to the hostess. I thought to myself, *Never again will I bring anything to this house.*

Michael and I sat at the dining room table watching as family members arrived for the dinner. The adults were greeted with an alcoholic drink of their choice, and Jim was kissing Erin's daughter, Kathy, up and down her neck and around to her semi-naked back, which made us feel very awkward. The way she was delighting in his greeting, we thought to ourselves that this was very unusual behavior for a daughter and stepfather. And when Stefan followed suit in greeting his sister in the same fashion and then touching her in places inappropriate for a Thanksgiving

Dinner get-together, we began seeing the signs of some sort of incestuous relationship going on there. However, we went into denial mode and thought perhaps that we had somehow misunderstood what was really happening.

As the dinner progressed, we all enjoyed pleasant conversation. As people made their way to the dessert, it was quite apparent that everyone truly enjoyed my special treat and began to compliment me on my cooking skills. Erin just fumed. It was stupendously perceptible that she was all puffed up and seething. It never occurred to me that she would get so furious that I had brought a dessert for all to enjoy. More than likely it was because the compliments that I received took away her thunder and praise. She quickly attempted to trivialize the compliments by starting an unrelated conversation that shifted the emphasis back to her.

Erin boasted, "I've always tried to be a good mother to my children and provide them with a good male role model to be a positive influence for them, you know, someone they called 'daddy' in their lives. My daughter is such a good person and appreciated everything I did for her, but my son just does not understand all the sacrifices I've made for him, and he remains defiant. I have worked very hard to keep him on a straight and narrow path." The conversation got a little old after a while, and we did not stay to help them clean up after the meal. We all left, and Stefan came with us. One could not help but wonder what was really going on in this family.

There were so many more red-flag instances of behavior that we, for some reason, chose to deny. It was the most difficult thing in the world for us to attempt to make a judgment about their family. There will always be a question of making judgment in error. Perhaps it was an evaluation made in haste and not representative of a person or situation at all. So I believe, out of fundamental fairness, we chose denial. And after all, when Stefan was with Melinda and her family, he was the consummate gentleman. He was reserved, charming, and very soft spoken.

We were also invited by Stefan to his mother's house for Christmas Eve. We always reserved Christmas Eve for our family, as it has always been an important and special day for us. It was the day for our family alone, and it was so special that we actually celebrated Christmas on Christmas Eve. We opened our presents and socialized with family. However, Stefan insisted that it was important for us to attend his mother's celebration, and we did not want to disappoint Stefan and Melinda and their budding relationship.

Stan and Gwen were also there. We had no idea at this time that these were their only friends. I brought presents for everyone in the family out of respect and appreciation for having been invited to their Christmas Eve gala. Jim was of Portuguese descent, and their celebration on the eve was a big fish-filled event. They went to a lot of effort in their cooking and presented a beautiful meal, and we felt honored to be sharing this evening with them. Before the meal commenced, Jim announced, "Please limit yourself to only one of everything."

Shortly after that announcement, Erin, knowing that I had brought gifts, announced, "There will be no opening of gifts this evening, as my children and grandchildren have been brought up to believe that Santa brings all gifts after midnight. Therefore, nothing will be opened until tomorrow morning." This was quite contrary to my Christian beliefs; however, we were in her house, and I respected her wishes.

There was some good conversation among all who attended, and there was some conversation as to who would be invited to the couple's wedding. Stefan and Melinda had prepared a list and asked his mother for names of people who were her friends and family they might want to add to that list. She became enraged and remarked, "No one would want to come to your wedding."

Michael and I managed a quick look at one another in affirmation of how uncomfortable we were beginning to feel. We both had the sense that something was amiss in this home and with the son getting married. After all, he was thirty-five years old and had never been married. But was there some reason why? There was much tension in that home after that, and, once again, we decided not to help with the dishes and went home to have our usual celebration. Stan and Gwen also decided to leave. Prior to us leaving, Erin gave presents to them and their children, and they all proceeded to open them. I began to wonder about this woman—did she have different agendas for different people? Once their presents were opened, they left. I picked up my presents and handed them to the appropriate people and said that we brought these gifts for them and that they could open them whenever they deemed it appropriate. When I handed Jim his gift, he opened it immediately.

We wished them all a Merry Christmas, hugged them, and left. We could not wait to get out of that house. We were feeling very uneasy about these people but shrugged it off as pre-wedding jitters, holiday stress, or what have you. Just because people don't do things the way we do doesn't make them abnormal—just different. However, as we watched their family dynamic play out before our very own eyes in the courtship phase of this relationship, I was convinced that this was certainly not a family dynamic that I would want to emulate for my own family.

We came home pleased as punch that we had survived the ordeal of Christmas Eve. We arrived home, and Stefan, Melinda, my husband, and I proceeded to celebrate in our own traditional fashion. We sat around in good conversation, we could eat very little, as we had more than our fill at the "in-laws'" house. We sat around talking about the upcoming wedding plans and opened gifts that we all had for each other. It was enjoyable, and the mood was jovial, and we all had a good time. We all celebrated Christmas together the next day, and all of my family came to my home for dinner.

Before any of the guests arrived, Stefan plopped a big kiss on my cheek and gave me a big old bear hug and told me, "I truly love your cooking, and I really enjoy being with you because there's nothing you can't do. I've never met anyone like you in my life." I was a good positive influence on him, and we enjoyed being and doing things together. His confidence in me was truly pleasing. He put my number in his cell phone and listed me as "Mom2." It was a warm and endearing gesture. "You know, my mother is not a warm person. She was very controlling and ridiculed her children and did not encourage them to try different things in life. She was possessive and opinionated, and her word was always the final say." I sensed his sincerity in what he was saying, and it made me feel warm and fuzzy all over. I knew in my heart that we were going to have a perfect family together. We became close, and he shared many personal moments with me both about his family and about himself.

I saw in him an awkward vulnerability and an inability to be independent. He always needed someone to be with him, either supporting him emotionally or working with him in a physical project. He seemed to me to be very childlike at times and, although a man, dependent and searching for acceptance. It was clear that he wanted to be an adult and a man, but he didn't know how. His mother was certainly of no help in dealing with his poor self-esteem. Everything in his life was a challenge. Everything was open to criticism. Everything needed confrontation in a he-said-she-said dialogue. Life was very complex in always getting to the bottom of things. I did not see this as a productive way to carry on his adult life, but maybe I was missing something in their relationship.

As the relationship continued for the couple, my husband and I were still in denial, overlooked the signs of something abnormal going on in Stefan's life, and continued with the wedding plans. We tried to include Erin in the plans and the organization of the wedding. The one time that she did come with us to order flowers, she arrived so late that we had already finished looking and ordering by the time she showed up. We took her out for dinner that evening, but she just sat there the whole time and told us how wonderful her daughter Kathy was. This was her son's wedding—what about him? Her praise continued *ad nauseum*. The only thing good about that evening was that she paid the check. We never invited her again to participate in any of the continuing planning.

It was only a short time from the meeting to the marriage. It was hectic but a great deal of fun to plan and organize such an affair. I dreamed about this day all my life, just the way little girls dream about their own wedding day. I wanted everything to be perfect and elegant for them. I dreamed about the life they could build together, the dreams they could realize, how beautiful their children would be, and what a wonderful life it would be for everyone. Melinda and I began walking two miles each day on the bike path to get in shape for the coming event. It was an important time in her life, and the walking in the blackness of the morning lent itself to a profound bonding and sharing of intimate events on both sides. Five o'clock every morning we were out there without fail, and then we would come home and shower and go to work. Melinda worked for the state for child protective services. She made a good living and had terrific benefits. Stefan was an electrician, and, although he made decent money, he did not stay at any employer for any length of time. He always had a story of how the other guys picked on him because he worked better than them, was more productive, was bald, or whatever it was. We never really gave his inability to hold a job a second thought. Little did we know that it would turn out to be, in retrospect, a red flag.

With such a whirlwind romance and everyone being caught up in the energy of this fairytale, it was easy not to notice an incident that popped up just prior to the wedding day. Melinda and Stefan had a disagreement and an altercation ensued. On the morning before the incident occurred I could feel the tension in the air. I could feel the quiet surrounding the house where they lived. It was very unusual because their house was a constant flurry of activity. However, inside the house was a much different story.

Stefan could be heard yelling, "My mother doesn't want me to marry you! She doesn't approve of you, and my sister doesn't like the way you dress!"

Melinda would yell back, "Grown men develop lives of their own and don't get a mother's permission to marry or pass muster of the family for someone they love!"

The bantering went back and forth for quite some time before Stefan stormed out of the house and went drinking with his buddies. They spent the day at the watering hole, and Melinda took a drive to the beach to be alone and to try and figure a way to not have Stefan's mother and sister be the decision makers in their married life. After all, Stefan was old enough to make decisions for himself and be confident in his decision to be supportive of the person he married, no matter what his family thought.

The house became eerily quiet with both of them out doing their own thing, but I knew that come evening, either this argument would have blown over, or we were experiencing the calm before the storm. Melinda arrived home first and poured herself a glass of wine to await Stefan's return. When he arrived home later that evening, he was in a foul mood. The argument from earlier that morning continued, but it was now fueled by alcohol. The screaming from that house was deafening, and I walked over and rang their doorbell just as Stefan, in a fit of rage, picked up the wooden framed end table in their living room and hurled it at Melinda. As the table sailed across the room in Melinda's direction, the glass portion disconnected from the wooden frame and the point at the corner of the glass skimmed across her arm as the frame fell to the floor. Melinda was in shock and disbelief that Stefan would do such a thing. With her arm bleeding, she called the police for assistance.

Realizing that Melinda called the police and my presence, Stefan became complacent and went into the bedroom and closed the door. The police came and took a statement from Melinda. She was hysterical and crying uncontrollably. The police asked, "Did you have anything to drink today?" She answered in the affirmative and told them she had just sat down with a glass of wine.

That was all they needed to hear. They then went into the bedroom and took a statement from Stefan. He told them a much different story than what actually happened when he told the police that Melinda had assaulted him, and he had a small red pressure spot on his cheek, from where he was laying on the pillow, to prove it. The police asked Stefan, "Did you have anything to drink today?"

Stefan said, "No, I just got home, and she assaulted me, so I went into the bedroom and closed the door to get away from her." Because Stefan did not tell the truth, Melinda got arrested for domestic violence. She was led away in handcuffs, processed through the police department for arraignment, and released later that evening. Stefan went to the police department, left the money for her bail, and moved in with his sister, because he was issued a restraining order against Melinda. The next day Stefan, after sobering from the previous night, called me and was very apologetic and asked what he could do to make this all go away. His mother, on the other hand, called me and for more than an hour tried to convince me that my child belonged in jail for what she did to her child. My position on the whole situation was that these two people were thirty-five years old, it was their lives, and we had no business being involved. They could figure this all out for themselves. Then she went one step further. She remarked that she would not allow her child to marry my daughter. This woman had some pretty serious control issues. Stefan and I worked together on getting this matter resolved favorably.

Her son was an adult and should be leaving his mother's control and establishing a family of his own. Would she also be involved in running his family too? I thought to myself that they had a disagreement, and this was a little extreme behavior for something as minor as a pre-wedding quarrel. I decided that they certainly did not deserve any intervention from me.

"Melinda, you know that marriage is such a huge commitment. Are you sure you want to continue with the marriage plans?"

Melinda smiled at me and said, "Mom, Stefan and I love each other very much, and he really needs to learn how deal with his mother. He is an adult, but he has never been allowed to be an adult. He needs to work on having an adult relationship not only with his mother but with other adults. We are going to get some counseling and work on the issue of his mother. His mother will have to learn some boundaries when it comes to her married children. She will have to learn to relinquish her control."

Melinda, "I just want you to think about it and look at it from all perspectives. A bad marriage is no piece of cake."

To which Melinda responded in her usual way, "Oh, Mom… you were married once before."

To which I replied, "Yes, I know, and I speak with experience!"

It was not such a minor event for Stefan's family, and they made that perfectly clear. Kathy now refused to be in her brother's wedding. It was purely out of common courtesy that his family was invited to the bridal shower. On the day of the bridal shower, although I was not expecting his mother or sister to show up, I was surprised when Erin, Kathy, and Gwen showed up and sat at one of the tables. The three of them were long faced, and Erin had on her plastic smile. All of the people who participated and enjoyed the bridal shower were my family and friends and Melinda's family, friends, and coworkers. The now-solo maid of honor and I hosted it. It was held at a new country club set way off in the woods, and it was beautiful and elegant, and it was a perfect day, and Melinda received many wonderful gifts with which to start her married life.

At the end of the shower I flitted around to all the tables and chatted with the guests who were kind enough to attend. I even went over to Erin's table, where she sat with Kathy and Gwen, shunning all other guests, and asked, "Did you have enough to eat? Please help yourselves if you would like more." I smiled a very uncomfortable smile the entire time I was interacting with them. Erin maintained her plastic smile throughout the event and continued as I left the table. The three of them chipped in for some token gift. I made a particular point to showcase this item and how kind it was for them to think so highly of their son in pooling their resources for such a fine gift. Other guests knowing the situation thought I was being way too kind. When they were ready to leave, they never said farewell to anyone; they just walked out. They did not acknowledge the bride-to-be, or the maid of honor, or the mother of the bride, or Stefan, who was also in attendance.

The wedding took place as planned in spite of everything that could go wrong actually going wrong and his mother complaining all afternoon that she didn't get any flowers. Unfortunately, the minister's daughter accepted the flowers that were being delivered to the church. She was a rotund, smiling, round-faced young woman who was obviously mentally challenged. When I confronted her after the ceremony, she admitted to receiving the flowers, but, not knowing what to do with them, she brought them into her house. It was an absolutely honest mistake, and she was frightened that she did something wrong. I felt terrible for having confronted her on behalf of Stefan's mother.

The weather on the wedding day was just awful. I quietly prayed that it would not be an omen of how the marriage would progress. It was blustery, cold, and rainy. No outdoor pictures were possible because of the constant downpour of rain and high wind. After taking indoor pictures throughout the country club, the wedding party was sequestered to an upstairs resting room, where they were served fresh seafood and drinks until it was time for the reception and the introduction of the bride and groom. This secret room was off limits to all guests, including the mother of the groom and her spouse, to ensure that they would not cause any tension between the bride and groom and that the day would flow smoothly. It was a safeguard that proved to be worth its weight in gold.

The reception room was magical with its fiery crystal chandeliers and greenery along a ceiling shelf interspersed and glistening like diamonds with twinkling white lights. The tables were draped in cream and white linens with optical crystal cylinder center pieces filled with water on which a flat, white candle, lit and floating, shot sparkling beams of light in all directions as the flame played off the breaks of optical glass. The bar was open, and the mood was merry. Before long the day was over, and it was a new beginning for this happy couple.

It was only after they married and got pregnant on the honeymoon that we began to see the real Stefan. Stefan's unbridled fury was released against Melinda, my husband, and me, and we have been living a nightmare ever since.

The Pregnancy and Birth

2006

Snow was coming down heavily, and the wind was howling fiercely, and we were officially in the middle of a blizzard. Some years we hardly got any snow, but this year, it was February 11, 2006, and we had whiteout conditions. I was chilled to the bone and was thinking to myself that Melinda's baby was several weeks overdue. Today, I was sure, would be the day that her baby would be born—guaranteed. As I was thinking about things, my telephone rang, and it was Melinda. "Mom, how do you know if your water has broken?"

I explained it all to her, and she confirmed that she was indeed in labor. I pried answers to certain questions from her. I asked her, "Do you have any pains or contractions?"

She replied, "No, I don't have any, and I feel perfectly fine."

I said, "Good. Please call the hospital and speak with them and tell them what is going on. Then depending on what they say, relax, take a nice warm shower and leisurely get ready so that you and Stefan and I can drive to the hospital."

The hospital was only a few miles away, but with whiteout conditions, it would take us some time to get there. It would be very slow going. A call explaining the situation to the hospital got a response of "get here as soon as you can." I said to her, "They know it'll take us some time to get there, so let Stefan help you get ready. Above all, stay calm. If you had contractions, and they were only minutes apart, then we would have to hurry. But this is your first child, and we have plenty of time." Stefan, of course, was of no help; he got hyper about everything. He was falling all over himself with nonsensical suggestions. "Stefan, please try to calm down, relax, and help your wife get ready. Do whatever she asks of you. Don't ask any questions—this is your child who's about to be born—you can help this child by helping your wife." I realized that he had never been a father before and this was all new to him. Of course he did not know what to do.

While waiting for Melinda and Stefan to make the final preparations for the birth of their child, I was relaxing on the couch reading my newspaper, close to the telephone, waiting for the phone call. I thought back to the beginning of the pregnancy. *It doesn't seem possible that it's already time for the birth. Where did those nine months go? Why, it seemed like only yesterday that we found out that we were to be blessed with another grandchild.*

With Melinda's job working for the state and the great health coverage they had, coupled with the generous maternity leave, they wouldn't have to pay for a thing. She decided to work right up until the last minute so that all of her maternity leave would be spent with her child. She would be able to stay home with her child for the first two years of life, and she would be able to breastfeed, make her own homemade baby food, and do all the things for this child that she had dreamed of. She had spent the last thirteen years taking care of the state's children that were neglected and unwanted or fell victims to drug-abusing parents. It made her really strong in her convictions about what a child, a baby in particular, really needed to grow into a productive adult. And since she lived right next door to her parents, she would have help at a moment's notice. It was such a perfect scenario. She had truly been blessed. We had all been blessed.

It was great fun for me to go shopping for maternity clothes for my child. I was a little in awe as to how much maternity clothing had changed since the days when I had my children. The latest trend was to wear tighter tops and accentuate that growing bulge, "baby bump," as it was now called. Bottoms were a big cutout and fit under the belly. It didn't seem comfortable to me, but I had no control over what was being manufactured and considered fashionable.

It had been a fairly easy pregnancy, and we took great pride in watching her waistline expand in size. I thought it was going to be (or at least I hoped with all my heart that it would be) a girl. I was not even willing to explore the possibility that it could be a boy.

There was so much to be done. We needed to plan the nursery and stock up with baby clothes, diapers, etc. Stefan and Melinda explored possibilities for a theme for the new arrival's room. After the exhaustive search of all possible themes, they finally decided on "Snuggle Bugs." The amazing part was that it had been a mutual decision. Thank goodness, now we at least had a theme to work with. I would redo their spare room in that theme and plan a baby shower in the same theme.

I loved my family so much, and it was a real honor to be involved in such an undertaking. Stefan and I decided that we did not want his child crawling around on the carpeting that had covered the floors in the apartment in which they lived and in which other people had previously lived. Stefan and I went on a binge and decided to rip up all the carpeting and put in laminate flooring. It started out with just the baby's room, but it didn't seem right to do just one room, as this child would be everywhere eventually. So on we continued and did the living room and closet and their bedroom, and when we were done, we decided that this little child should have a new floor in the kitchen, laundry room, and bathroom. There was no stopping us now. It was truly a family effort, and we had a lot of fun doing that project.

Stefan and I worked really well together. We enjoyed doing the same things and took great delight in every precious moment we spent in remodeling the apartment so that his child could have a superb welcoming home. It was also a great way for me to get to know Stefan even better and for him to truly see the family of which he was now a part. It was the perfect mechanism for bonding for both him and I and the blending of two families. He shared with me much of his personal life, some prior to the wedding, about his mother being a person who did not tell the truth to either of her children. Neither was she interested in nurturing her children nor in helping them develop their talents in a positive way so that they could become productive members of society.

We thought we were only going to walk our two miles a day until we had lost enough weight to fit into our wedding clothing. Wrong! Now we were going to continue our walking for the health of this child she was carrying. It was a little cold in the wintertime, but when there was no snow covering the path, we were committed to this child. We watched that belly grow on a daily basis. And when the day came that there was movement from within, it was such a momentous happening.

She signed us up for every baby care and baby product seminar that she could find. It was as if she thought that I had never had a baby before. We participated at every one of them, and it was just amazing to see how the technology had evolved from my childrearing days. The real fun was in planning the baby shower. She registered for everything she could find that was the Snuggle Bug theme, both online and at all the baby stores. It was hard to pick a date for the shower because the baby was due in February, and the date was always iffy at best. It could not be held in January because that was right after the holidays, and right before the holidays all the good places to have a shower were booked with holiday parties. I was forced to rent a hall at a local watering hole, and I was not too happy with that idea. However, being the resourceful person that I was, and with the help of some friends, we enveloped and transformed a dirty, old bar into a magical baby land. We had three hundred helium-filled balloons in purple, pink, and blue marking off the perimeter of a more cozy area of this large hall. We adorned each table with huge Christmas greens centerpieces in the same color scheme as the balloons, together with baby bottles, pacifiers, pins, and other baby items as well as Christmas balls, which were fastened on a large floral pick and stuck strategically in the centerpieces. Invitees were in awe of the transformation. The workers at the bar asked if we would leave the hall decorated when we were finished because it was so beautiful. They wanted to enjoy it for as long as they could. We were happy to comply.

Once the shower was over, our projects were rekindled and our list was never ending. And as our projects grew in number, so did Melinda's belly, and so did our excitement about a new baby. Melinda's belly and our to-do list were in constant competition.

Whenever we worked together on our projects, Stefan was forthcoming with many a sad story about his childhood. While we were working one Saturday morning, Stefan became very sullen and teary-eyed. He said to me, as he sat motionless on an overturned bucket of flooring glue, "Did you know that when I was about nine years old, my father told me one evening that he was going to kill himself that night? I became very upset about this possibility, and I immediately went to my mother, very afraid for my father's well-being, and I told her what my father had in mind. My mother told me that my daddy was a big boy and could do whatever he wanted. Sometime that evening, he rigged up a rope to the ceiling and placed the rope around his neck and jumped from the center island of his kitchen. I found him hanging in his kitchen the next morning. My mother didn't see the need for any therapeutic intervention for her children."

Stefan continued, "I still have that kitchen island that my father made and used to hang himself from." It was in the kitchen of the house that he now owns. He was so proud of it; he brought me over to his house to show it to me. It was as if this were some sort of prize—a trophy. It was all that he had left of his father and a very sad remembrance of their final visit together. I believe he told me this because he wanted me to feel his pain.

As we sat there in his kitchen and he looked at me with eyes that were black and vacant, I not only saw and felt his pain, but I could also visualize the actions and panic that this young child experienced in such a gruesome manner. My heart went out to this nine-year-old boy, who was now a thirty-five-year-old man, who was now to become a father himself. Instead of his mother tending to the emotional needs of her children, he and his sister were left alone often while his mother was out looking for the next husband that her children would be calling "Daddy."

One day, during our morning walks, Melinda confided that Stefan's behavior had become somewhat violent in nature since their marriage. It was not a constant situation, but it had been escalating. As she was talking, events started to crystallize, and I realized that Stefan had been pretending all this time. He had anger and control issues stemming from the lack of any sort of therapeutic intervention for the anger he was repressing over the death of his father. Now that they were married and were having a baby, he no longer had to control or suppress any of it. He was free to unleash it.

Piecing together the bits of information that Melinda and I shared during our daily trek into the blackness of pre-dawn and all of the information Stefan had shared with me personally while we were working on our never ending projects, I realized that Stefan was the product of a very unhappy and lonely childhood. There were some very subtle nuances from time to time that gave me that sinking feeling inside that perhaps I should not have overlooked and paid a little more attention. Stefan would tell me something, and the way he said it, the tendency was to believe him because he was a part of our family, but deep in my gut I didn't really believe what he was saying.

He had suffered a frontal lobe brain injury as a rebellious teenager, and now, as an adult, these past experiences were keeping him from functioning as a responsible husband. He and Melinda would have a disagreement about something, and he would always find it necessary to come to me and explain himself so that Michael and I would not think poorly of him. Every conversation would end with a quasi-apology and a promise to never hurt Melinda and most of all to love her forever. It always reminded me of something that he had rehearsed in front of a mirror.

I always believed what he told me, but there was always that underlying doubt gnawing away inside. The natural progression of things was to try to get him some help. We knew of a neurologist who was a tremendous and positive influence in helping a family member who had sustained a serious brain injury. Surprisingly, when I confronted Stefan with what I knew, he was receptive and displayed a sense of relief that someone could see his pain and was eager to go to see this doctor for help.

My daughter made the appointment, and they both went to see the doctor who, after numerous visits and many diagnostic tests, made a diagnosis and prescribed medication. The transformation was phenomenal. He was like a different person. He was calm, loveable, family-oriented, focused, and a real joy to be around and interact with. The doctor also suggested he connect with a therapist for positive reinforcement while working out his anger issues. The joy, however, was short lived.

As soon as he told his mother, she immediately ordered him to stop taking the medication because we were making him into a "yes man," and we were trying to control him. He immediately stopped taking the medication in order to please his mother. Once the medication was completely out of his system, he reverted back to his controlling and abusive behavior. Even though all of his abuse, anger, and hostility were toward Melinda and her family, we still had projects that needed to be completed before this child came into the world. Our working together had become a real challenge, and Stefan's involvement was more hit or miss, and I, for the most part, now worked without his help.

Our last major project on the list was for the décor of the child's room. We had to remain neutral. We still didn't know if it was a boy or a girl. The room was painted purple. Purple was a mix of pink and blue—you can't get any more middle of the road than that. We put up a Snuggle Bug border. I cut out some of the Snuggle Bugs left over from the border and randomly pasted them on the walls. The switch plate covers were covered in Snuggle Bug paper. The room was very bright and colorful, just like babies like. I remained determined to finish all our projects before the little one made an appearance.

We cleaned, washed, and scrubbed, and we painted the entire apartment. We wanted only the best for this child. We all wanted it germ free and sparkling. Halfway through the pregnancy and halfway through all of our projects, Melinda posed the question: "Mom, how much do you know about a 'doula'?"

I thought she might be some sort of cleaning woman, but, to my surprise, I was informed that a doula was a woman who assists the mother during the pregnancy and was in the delivery room helping with the birth. I had never heard of such a thing other than midwifery. Melinda told me this was part of natural childbirth, and this was what she wanted, so I had to bring myself up to speed! Not wanting my baby, who was having her own baby, to be disappointed, I immediately got on the Internet and found out this was very popular with pregnant women who took the holistic approach to childbirth. So I bought a book to bring myself up to speed, as she called it. It was exhausting reading coupled with all my projects getting ready for the baby, but anything that my child wanted to make this delivery easier on her I would be willing to do.

Finally, around ten that morning, I got the anticipated phone call. Melinda called and said, "Mom, are you ready? Because Stefan and I are ready for the drive to the hospital now." I packed a bag of munchies for my son-in-law and me so that we could keep up our strength, and I packed a six-pack of bottled water, although I was sure he would probably want something a lot stronger than that. I warmed the car so that no one would be cold, especially the anticipated new arrival. The wind was howling, and the snow was falling fast and furiously as we slowly made our way down the slippery stairs from her loft apartment. Ever so slowly, we inched our way along until we reached my vehicle. As we got out into the driveway, we could see the neighbors waving to us from their windows. The snow was very deep, and we took my vehicle because it had four-wheel drive, and there would be less of a chance of us getting stuck and possibly having an in-the-car delivery. It was very slow going. It had been at least two hours since she first called the hospital, and they told us to come as soon as we could.

We finally arrived safely. None of the parking lots were cleared of snow, so I pulled up to the door, and the mommy-to-be got out and went inside to wait for Stefan and I to park the car. We parked my SUV close by, and as we ran to the entrance of the hospital, I had the sense that I had not turned off my lights. Stefan ran back, looked, and told me that the lights were out.

We brought Melinda to the delivery room, and there was not one other person in delivery. They informed her that she could have any room of her choice. She picked the room with the pool in it because, in her research in birthing methods, she read that being in a pool of tepid water makes the contractions bearable, and this was quite important in a natural delivery. The nurses were quite wonderful and treated us all like family. They showed us where we could get snacks for ourselves or make tea or coffee, etc. The first thing Stefan wanted to do was make himself a hot chocolate.

As we were settling Melinda into the bed and getting her ready for examination by the doctor, Stefan busied himself, rearranging the lighting in the delivery room. He was not the least bit interested in helping his wife. I thought he was supposed to be her coach for this natural childbirth, but how was that going to be possible if he was checking out every light that did not work, or every bulb that was burned out and every electrical outlet that he deemed improperly installed? In this particular instance, there were a few drawbacks to being in the electrical profession. He was a very busy, busy person, but in a negative way.

Dr. Morgan arrived, and there was an instant rapport as he examined the mother-to-be and indeed confirmed that the water had broken. He announced, "She won't be leaving the hospital until she delivers." He ordered the nurses to administer an IV that would get the labor moving. We all sat around for the remainder of the day waiting for Melinda to go into hard labor and deliver this child. Finally, by suppertime, we were all hungry, and Stefan wanted Chinese food. Because we were in the middle of a blizzard, there were no restaurants open, and we had to call around to find a Chinese restaurant that could help us with our dilemma. When we finally found one that was open, Stefan and I went out to my car, only to find that the battery was dead. The lights were not off, and now I had to find someone who would jump my battery in the middle of a blizzard in order to go and get some Chinese food. Being the eternal optimist and ever so resourceful, I called my husband, who took Melinda's SUV and came to the hospital and jumped my battery, and off we all went to a Chinese restaurant for takeout. We brought back plenty of food so that everyone could partake, including Melinda, who still had not had a contraction. We all laughed, joked, and ate heartily.

The doctor checked on Melinda several times during the evening, and she was still minimally dilated. This little baby was going to take his sweet time coming into this world. He liked the safety and security of his mommy's belly. Everyone in the delivery was just as kind and helpful as could be.

"However," the nurse explained to me, "it's around midnight, and you should go home and get some sleep and be fresh for tomorrow, as this is when Melinda will really need you. This baby will not be born this evening—guaranteed." I did not want to leave my child, but I did take the nurse's advice. Melinda was in good spirits and believed what the nurse was telling us. After all, Stefan would be there with her if anything should happen. I thought I could best help my child if I were well rested. As I walked out to my vehicle, I noticed that the snow had slowed considerably and the flakes were much smaller in size. The wind had subsided, and the ride home was quick.

Sleep came very easily that evening, as I was exhausted from the day's events. That sleep was greatly needed, and I did not want to get up in the morning. When I finally did arise, I did not rush. I fortified myself with a good breakfast, leisurely showered, and then left for the hospital. I would not be coming back to my house until that child was born.

When I saw Melinda for the first time, the contortion of her body told me she was now in real labor. I kissed her on the forehead, and she said, "I started with contractions the previous night, and they kept injecting me with medication to keep the contractions strong. I'm exhausted from dealing with the pain and contractions all night. I want it to be over."

I thought to myself, *I feel your pain, and there's not a thing I can do to help it.* The entire day consisted of contraction after contraction, but the dilation process was very slow, and it was very obvious that this child was not even attempting to move down the birth canal. I stayed by her side and wiped her brow of sweat and rubbed her feet and her body that ached, and we were riding out this labor together. Stefan was out looking at electrical anomalies, or so he thought. He did not give a second thought to his wife or unborn child. He was always off tinkering with some electrical situation and not knowing what to do on a personal level, just avoided the entire birthing process.

I truly believed that we would make progress that day and that the child would be born soon. But, on the evening of the second day, the doctor announced that she still had not dilated sufficiently, and the baby had not moved any farther down the birth canal. My son-in-law was oblivious to what birth was all about and was quite annoyed that the child had not been born yet. That evening they ramped up the labor inducement drugs and put Melinda into hard labor. I was with her all night, mopping her brow and squeezing her hand and rubbing whatever part of her body that she requested to be rubbed to relieve the pain and soreness. I cannot even begin to count the number of cups of ice that we went through in order to cool her down and make the pain bearable.

Stefan slept in a chair and slept like a baby and the next morning could not figure out why I was helping *his* wife all night. He could not understand why his wife was not all hugs and kisses just by the mere fact that he was there with her going through this with her. Stefan was certainly a different breed of animal. "Wake me if anything happens," he instructed.

All night long she pushed with every contraction, and she sweated, and I mopped and rubbed, and we thought our all-night endeavors would surely render a favorable decision by the doctor when he arrived in the morning.

At ten o'clock in the morning of the third day of labor, the doctor arrived and checked Melinda by internal examination. He looked at Melinda and he looked at me and he shook his head. "She's now only three centimeters dilated, and the baby still hasn't moved down the birth canal," he announced.

Melinda strongly told the doctor, "I can't endure any more."

The doctor agreed, "I'll let you go for one hour longer, and if you haven't progressed significantly, I'll perform a C-section." So on she went with hard labor. Stefan was off on one of his electrical adventures and then went to get himself some break-fast. I continued talking my child through the contractions and mopping her soaking brow. My happiest moment was when she looked up at me through a face full of beaded sweat and said, "Mom, thank you for being here with me and helping me!"

Tears of joy rolled down my tired and red-flushed face. I said to her, "I've always been here for you. You're my child; I will be there always for you until the day they put me in the ground." We both hugged and told each other how much we loved each other.

After the hour had passed and after examination by the doctor, it was decided that a C-Section would be performed. Melinda had been in labor for three days, and it would be pru-dent to bring the child into the world by some way other than a vaginal delivery. The doctor came bustling back into the room and announced that the operating room was free and this child was going to be born. It was Valentine's Day—what a perfect day for a birthday. February 14, 2006—I was sure my "granddaughter" was going to come into the world today. Only the father would be allowed in the operating room, and I eagerly sat in the birthing room waiting for some news. One nurse popped her head in and informed me it was a boy! I was in denial. *What does she know?* And then Stefan came in and delightedly informed me that it was a boy. I was in disbelief. I wanted a girl so badly, but I guess that was not to be, at least not this time. I needed to deal with the fact that I was the proud grandmother of a little boy named Bryce.

After I held this precious bundle of joy for a few minutes and "ohhed" and "ahhed" all over him, I handed him over to his parents, and I went home. I never returned to the hospital to visit with them. I had been there for three days with little to no sleep and now would be the time for me. I knew that other friends and family would be visiting, and it made perfect sense for me to stay home and relax and catch up on some sleep and wait for the moment when this little bundle of joy would come home. When they all came home in a few days, we would all begin the family phase of our lives.

The Homecoming

2006

Waiting and ready with camera in hand when the big day arrived, I could barely contain my excitement. The new arrival was now a week old and just as perfect as could be. But I could tell something was wrong, and my joy quickly turned to fear and apprehension as I watched Melinda's face and actions. Stefan's actions spoke louder than any words, and what he vocalized was even more shocking. I was standing on the balcony of their second floor apartment, watching as Stefan took the baby out of the car and held him ever so close to his body as he brought him up the stairs and placed him on their bed and then went about household endeavors. I had been so full of excitement, but when I realized that he took the baby and had not given his wife a second thought, I became very upset with Stefan's actions. She was still outside desperately trying to navigate the long stairway unaided.

"Melinda, wait, hold on, I'll come and help you!" I shouted to her. I ran down the stairs to assist her in climbing the fifteen steps to the landing. When we got to the top, Stefan was standing there with a scowl on his face. Stefan looked boldly at me and said, "There's no need for you to come in. I can handle things here." I was crushed, and my heart was broken as tears began to roll down my face. I kept my distance from that house and only went over after Stefan had left for work after his two-week paternity leave. What was it that could have altered our relationship so drastically? He had shared so much of his personal life with me during our baby remodeling projects. I was completely in the dark, but I was quite certain that the operative word here was *mother.*

In our bonding phase, Stefan shared a good amount of negativity about his mother. Erin was very close to her own mother. She had a brother, and both his mother and grandmother were very critical of any woman he ever dated or considered marriage material. When he did marry, both women set about to do everything and anything possible to end that marriage. The brother, being an upstanding and well-balanced human being, chose his wife over his family and moved to California. He had nothing to do with his mother or his sister and had a wonderful marriage and happy and healthy children.

Stefan's mother and grandmother did the same thing to him. They did not like any girl he dated, was romantically involved with, or considered marrying. There was always something that did not pass muster with his family. Consequently, he went from woman to woman to woman, trying to please his family. Prior to Stefan and Melinda's marriage, he decided to strike out on his own and lived in several different areas of the country in order to prove his independence and his manhood. He moved to numerous cities in Alabama, where his life was less than ideal. He was ill-equipped to successfully forge a life for himself without his mother telling him what he needed to do.

His independence was short lived in that state. Subsequently, he moved to various cities in California so that he could be near family at a very minimum. He enrolled in a community college and worked in a group home to support himself. This endeavor was also short lived, as he was fired for physically assaulting a handicapped woman in his charge. His next move was back home to his mother. And it was only when he started calling me "Mom" that his mother went into overdrive to destroy his marriage.

We desperately tried to keep Stefan a viable member of our family and to help him sort out and deal with whatever demons were plaguing him. Our walks continued when Stefan was working. We would bundle up Bryce and go for our "zoom, zoom" as we lovingly termed our walks with the child. He would take his morning nap, and we got the benefit of the two-mile walk. Melinda shared bits and pieces of her life with me as we walked. After she divulged the verbal vulgarities that he bestowed upon her each day, I also began to notice bruises on her body and noticed that he would be out late at night or sometimes not even bother to come home at all. Melinda tried very hard to hold their new family together, but it was obvious that things were quite different. She told me that when she was in the hospital and Kathy had come to visit, he took the baby from Melinda and placed him in Kathy's arms and said "smile at mommy" as he took a picture.

Melinda let her mind run wild as to what he meant by that statement. Were the rumors of incest in that family true? It wasn't long after their arrival home to begin life as a threesome before Stefan announced to Melinda while she was making his breakfast and packing him a nice lunch one morning, "You know, I don't love you. I never loved you. I am, as a matter of fact, in love with my sister."

Melinda had been sucker punched and was unable to deal with what Stefan was telling her. *What on earth is he talking about?* she thought. She was at a loss for words. She was immobilized by fear and the meaning of Stefan's words. She thought long and hard about her marriage and what the impact of his words would have on their marriage.

At a time when hormones are raging after just giving birth and now this bomb being dropped on her, it was hard to stay focused. It was hard to think of what was really important. But the more she and I talked about it and thought about things, it started to become abundantly clear to us that Kathy's daughter looked exactly like Stefan and nothing like her husband. And now, Kathy would have a son with her brother too. The possibilities of what was really going on here were endless, and we could not help but think about the greetings we experienced at Stefan's mother's house during the holidays of the previous year between Kathy and the stepfather and between Kathy and her brother.

"Mom, what can I do?" she begged. "I don't want my marriage to fail. I love my husband, and I thought that we were going to be helpmates to each other, and we would prosper and be happy."

I could feel her despair and rejection. There was nothing I could say that would change any of this for her. I believe it was at this point that we all began to look at Stefan in a different light and really begin to take note of all the red flags that we were so unwilling to recognize in the short time from the engagement to the birth of the child. My heart went out to Melinda, knowing that she now had some very serious soul searching to do and some very serious decisions to make. Days turned into weeks, and weeks into months, and we all walked on eggshells in order to avoid the wrath of Stefan. We did not know for sure what was going on and could only let our imaginations take over in pure speculation as to this change in his behavior.

Melinda confided that he called her the most awful names imaginable, such horrible vulgarities that she had never heard before, and the list went on and on. When his baby was three months old, he decided to play with him after work one day when he graced them with his presence and picked up the baby by the legs and then forcefully flung him up over his head. "Stefan!" I forcefully yelled, "What are you doing with your child? You cannot do that to such a young child. You could seriously injure or even kill that baby. What you are doing is called 'shaken baby syndrome' and you need to stop!"

Stefan looked me square in the eyes with a sinister smirk on his face and said, "I can do whatever I want. I am this baby's father, and I will do whatever I please." I was very, very afraid for this child. He would come home from work and take off his dirty leather belt that he wore while crawling around people's dirty, dank basements and give it to his baby to chew and suck on. His actions and thoughtlessness were repulsive to me.

We tried to remain optimistic for the sake of this marriage and this child and tried in earnest to help Stefan. It was very clear to us that there was some sort of mental condition or anomaly that he was suffering. As the days went by, his behavior became more and more unbearable. We tried so desperately to talk with him and to see if there was something that we could help him work through, or if he was having any particular problems that we could help him identify and work through. We could talk it out and maybe advise him where to get help. He insisted that there was nothing wrong with him. His mother was always the first to confirm this for him.

Melinda, in the meantime, easily made that transition from her role as spouse to that of doting mother. She was very motherly and was truly enjoying motherhood. It became her. She had even purchased a "co-sleeper," which was a small crib with one side missing that snuggled right up to her bed so that Bryce could sleep with his parents. However, it only allowed one parent easy access to the child without any possible harm to baby that could conceivably happen if the child had slept directly in the bed with the parents. She welcomed that closeness to her child. Melinda spent her days pumping breast milk and cooking homemade baby food for her baby, and she dealt with Stefan's behavior in a positive way, encouraging him to become self-employed, as he was not able to hold down a job for very long. Everything his mother told him he could not do, Melinda reinforced that he could do it. She made his breakfast and coffee in the morning, packed his lunch daily, and always remembered to include a little note telling him how much he meant to her. She really and truly loved him.

We were desperate to help Stefan and Melinda work through their situation, and we were also very committed to giving this child as normal of a life as possible under the circumstances. I went to their house every day and fed him his breakfast and had a cup of tea with lemon in it. Before long, Bryce was also sharing that cup of tea with me.

During all of the bad times, there were also some memorable moments too. At five months old, Bryce went into the swimming pool and spent many hours outdoors by the pool with his mom and dad. He loved being in the water. Daddy was teaching him to swim. Daddy held his legs and moved them up and down in the water, telling him to "kick, kick, kick." When daddy let go of his legs and said "kick, kick, kick," his little legs began to move. It would not be long before he would be swimming on his own.

His baby book, which I worked on diligently for three years, was the most complete baby book anyone had ever seen. It was just jam-packed with his family history from birth to the age of three. It recorded many important milestones in his short life. I take great delight in remembering that at the ripe old age of five and a half months, he started drinking his water from a Poland Springs sports bottle and shared a bottle with his grandmother regularly. He could not resist. He loved water! At the age of six months, he started eating solid food three times a day. Mommy gave him toast. He made all kinds of faces, but he didn't quit. During one of his visits to grandma's house, he managed to pick up a six-pound cement pig from the living room coffee table and throw it on the floor and break its foot off. What strength in those chubby little hands!

Stefan was so consumed with anger and being abusive that he did not even notice that his child was attempting to crawl at the age of nine months. Or that he was able to shake his head "no." It was so funny to ask him something and watch him shake his head. Stefan missed so much of that child's life because he was so busy cussing and storming at his wife that he did not even realize that his child was in the room. His child heard all of the rage and the anger.

Christmas that year was exciting for us in spite of Stefan's behavior, as it was the baby's first Christmas. He was only ten months old and not at all into presents or Santa Claus. He just wanted to stick all the wrapping paper in his mouth. I made him a toy chest, gave him some lambskin slippers to keep his little feet nice and warm and oodles and oodles of socks and some new clothes. Mommy and Daddy got him a truck that he just loved to push along, and when he needed some attention, he blew the horn! He was such a smart little boy. The real Christmas present for us was when, just a few days later, he started standing in one spot all by himself (albeit for just a minute), but then just two days after that, he took two steps by himself. It scared the bejeebers out of him, and he sat down. It was very, very close now—there would be no stopping him.

We all really tried to stay focused on the upbringing of this child, and, in between time, we encouraged the child's father to get help so that the three of them could evolve into a loving, caring, and viable family filled with all the wants, needs, and desires of any normal family. Because of the parents' ages, they wanted another child in a short period of time. I begged them to work on their stability as a couple and their abilities to provide a loving and caring home with one child. I personally did not see much hope for them but tried to send forth positive energy.

Sometimes when Stefan was on his medication, he was a good person, loving, and interactive with his wife and his son. When his mother had her say, which was quite often, he would not take his medication, and he became like Dr. Jekyll and Mr. Hyde. We would notice the difference almost immediately. When the doctor prescribed the medication that allowed him to be almost human, the doctor also suggested counseling in conjunction with taking the medication. This, his mother was dead set against, and Stefan put it on the back burner for quite some time.

From all the negative things Stefan had shared with me about his family, I truly wanted to try to help him get the services necessary for him to turn his life around. I could sense from him all the rejection, isolation, and unanswered questioning and blame

Louise Baron-Kent

a young child experiences when a beloved family member commits suicide. I believe he was still carrying around all of that baggage from his childhood. He had built upon it and, in his own distorted way, wanted someone to take responsibility for what had happened to him during his youth. It was a daily struggle for everyone involved. Sometime in the early fall, much to our amazement, Stefan began seeing a therapist.

All of our hopes were high, and as we encouraged Stefan in his journey, we also prayed for a positive outcome.

Prelude to the End

Melinda accompanied her husband to the therapist that his neurologist recommended, and they explained to him that Stefan had been in a very serious automobile accident when he was a teenager. He was a passenger, with two other passengers, in the back seat of a motor vehicle driven by another teenager, who was killed instantly when the vehicle crashed, after a night of partying. Stefan suffered serious injuries and sustained a frontal lobe brain injury. Once he was released from the hospital after many weeks of inpatient care, his mother did not allow him to have any follow-up medical treatment. He attempted to deal with his mood swings, violent behavior, and bizarre actions by himself. His physical being was restored, but he was not even aware that his actions and mental functioning were inappropriate. It appeared that he tried very hard on a daily basis to control his inabilities by acting impulsively and quite inappropriately. He began treatment with Dr. Walsh, his neurologist, when he could no longer control his anger on his own. Dr. Walsh did much in the way of neurological testing and evaluating and found him to have an explosive personality disorder and to be suffering from attention deficit hyperactivity disorder (ADHD). Dr. Walsh placed Stefan on medication, which he took religiously for a short period of time. That was until the day he confided to his mother that he was taking medication, and he then began taking it in a "hit-or-miss fashion," whenever his mother did not intervene.

Melinda had been seeing a therapist of her own to help her work through and understand Stefan's abnormal and extraordinary behaviors. Her therapist was completely unaware that he had become physically abusive. Her therapist suggested couples' counseling. Melinda desperately wanted to explore this avenue, not only to help her husband but also to help put the marriage on a good course. They attended three sessions. Stefan was argumentative at all three sessions, and the therapist could clearly see that any further sessions would be counter-productive. He referred Melinda to another female therapist who specialized in domestic violence and encouraged her to help herself for a better understanding of her spouse.

Stefan's abusive behavior continued, and he was unrelenting in his violence toward his wife. We were very afraid for the safety of our daughter and our grandson. Shortly prior to his therapy session the first week of October 2006, Melinda had a restless night and had been mulling over in her mind everything about her marriage. Outward appearances demonstrated Stefan was such a demure, laid-back, and always willing-to-lend-a-hand-type of person. Reality was that if it was not in his best interest, there would be hell to pay. Melinda had enough of his physical and emotional abuse and decided that she was going to end her marriage and obtain a divorce from her husband.

Melinda struggled emotionally about having a failed marriage. She truly wanted the man to whom she was married to see what he was doing to their family. She wanted for him to take control of his life and make changes…to become her knight in shining armor. She desperately wanted the white picket fence and the happy little home and a loving and caring spouse. She wanted it all but was unable to figure out a way for her husband to see all the good she had to offer him.

She told him over breakfast that morning. Her stomach muscles ached from being taut, and it was difficult for her to breathe as she began to broach the subject of divorce. She did not want to be there and she did not want to do this. It took her many agonizing months to come to this conclusion. "Stefan," she began speaking ever so gently, "I really love you, and I thought that we would have a long and wonderful life together, you, me and our child, but since I have given birth to this child, you have changed. You are not the same person that I dated and certainly not the same person that I married. I am finding out all these not so pleasant things about you. I am learning from you that you have been sexually intimate with more than one thousand women. You admit to being in love with your sister. You have been fired from every employment situation you have had. You have no boundaries with your family. Your family makes decisions in your marriage. My head is just spinning. You are not at all the person that I thought I was marrying. I do not even know you, and I am guessing that I will never know you."

Stefan responded to her dissertation by picking up Melinda's belongings and throwing them on the floor in a fit of rage and smashing them all to bits. He did not speak to her. He just kept smashing her belongings. Melinda became hysterical and began yelling, "Stefan, please stop, our child is right here, and he is watching what you are doing. Please stop!" Stefan was too enraged to even hear what she was saying, and he continued his destruction until he was ready to stop. When he had finished, he walked out the door, leaving behind a household full of debris.

Melinda did not get to say all that she had to say. She barely hinted at the word *divorce*, but I guess he knew it was inevitable. This seemed to be the same scenario for every relationship he had ever been in. That was a monumental decision for her to make, as their baby was only eight months old, and she did not want him caught up in the middle of that ugliness.

She grew up without her biological father in her life, and she wanted something different for her son. Nothing was making any sense to her, and she could not comprehend how someone who was so close to her and supposedly loved her so much did a complete three-sixty in a matter of months. Once the dust had settled and they could once again speak to each other in a civilized manner, Melinda said to Stefan, "This is the moment of truth. I am filing for divorce. There is nothing further that you can say or do to change this. I do not want my son to see the things that you do to me. I still love you, and this is not what I want for us. But you have given me no other choice."

Stefan, stood there in the kitchen looking at Melinda with eyes that revealed emptiness and continued his look like he could control her with his stare and of course, true to his nature, berated her when she told him of her decision. Stefan screamed at her, "If you leave me, I will make your life a living hell." Stefan escalated into a higher pitched scream. "I will leave you with nothing. I will make sure that you will be destitute and begging for death when I am finished with you."

Melinda considered this to be an idle threat. "Men, real men, do not act this way toward their loving partner."

Once again, he started to throw her possessions around the house, breaking as much as he could get his hands on. And once again, he continued to shout vulgarities at her right up until the moment he slammed the door and left. The events of the last two days had been festering in him. His behavior in the evening would be a manifestation of those festering thoughts and feelings. Melinda was glad that he had left. She could not process his words and try and figure what her course of action should be.

Because Stefan had been so violent as of late, and because of his inability to think through situations in a rational manner, Melinda called his therapist and asked him to work with Stefan in preparing him for the divorce. That night would be different from all of his other counseling sessions. Stefan decided he was going to get even with his wife. He proceeded to paint a picture of his wife more heinous, vile, and depraved than anyone's wildest imagination. I did not know absolutely for sure, nor did Melinda know exactly what transpired during that meeting that afternoon, except that whatever Stefan told the therapist resulted in the therapist calling child protective services and filing a complaint to have the child removed immediately from its mother and placed in foster care. He not only called child protective services once, he called them several times within a short period of time and insisted that this was an emergency, and they needed to come immediately to remove the child. He repeatedly informed them that Melinda was an employee of child protective services. Not only did he want the child removed from the home, he made overt and aggressive representations to them as to place her employment in jeopardy. The therapist advised Stefan to go home and abduct that baby and get it as far away from the mother as he could.

We subsequently discovered that Stefan concocted a story about his wife being a hardcore alcoholic and given to being a down-in-the-gutter, hardcore drug-abusing woman who was breastfeeding their son and passing this evilness down to their child through the breast milk on a daily basis.

Stefan was extremely over the edge on his drive home. He flagged down a police cruiser he saw in the neighborhood and said excitedly, "You must come to my house and remove my child from its mother, because he is in danger!"

The police officer, who knew Stefan from town responded, "This will not be possible. You will need a court order for us to go into the home and pluck a child away from its mother. This is just not the role of the police department."

Stefan shot back abruptly, "She is a drunk and a drug addict, and you have to do this."

The police officer said in a very professional voice, "I am sorry, but I cannot help you."

One can only imagine what the police officer thought when Stefan told him that he was coming from therapy. And with what he wanted them to do, they must have thought that he was an absolute fruit loop. Stefan, even more excited than he was prior to stopping the police cruiser, had no choice but to continue on his way home.

My son-in-law arrived home that evening in an extremely excited and explosive state and became outrageously abusive and physically violent toward me, a senior citizen, his own child, and the child's mother. He damaged the property and smashed Melinda's possessions. He quickly began packing as much clothing as he could and told Melinda that child protective services would be coming for the child. Melinda, needless to say, was in shock and disbelief at what Stefan had done. He thought that if he created a tale of magnanimous proportions and got protective services involved, he would accomplish two things. First, he thought Melinda would lose her job because she worked for protective services, and second that they would give the baby to him to raise forever. Over, done—no questions asked.

What Stefan did not know was that this was not the way protective services worked. When a complaint was lodged, the child was removed and put immediately into foster care. Stefan, in his own demented thinking, actually thought that his child would be better off in the foster care system of the state government. He was gravely delusional and mentally unstable to do this to his own flesh and blood because he was mad at his wife and wanted to get even with her.

A shouting match ensued, and Melinda called me to her apartment to help with the situation. When I arrived, he was in their bedroom and haphazardly packing his bag. When I asked him to leave the premises, he flew into a rage and attempted to physically assault me. He came at me full bore with a closed fist so close to me that I could feel the movement of the air between his fist and my face. I was absolutely horrified, and my body was shaking uncontrollably, and I thought he was going to knock my teeth out.

In the split seconds of this threatening activity, I remembered thinking to myself, *If he doesn't kill me with that first blow, and I'm able to get up, it'll be all over for him. I will kill him!* I looked into his eyes, and all I saw was red, pure rage. I thought he was the devil personified! I had never experienced this intensity of horror with any other human being, ever in my life. He was in an uncontrollable fit of rage; however, he did manage to stop just a hair's breadth shy of delivering that blow and, instead, proceeded to kick a mirrored closet door so that it smashed into tiny shards of glass. He did not strike my face. I called the police, and Stefan was subsequently arrested on domestic violence and domestic vandalism charges that evening.

In my estimation, the therapist overstepped his bounds in making those desperate calls to child protective services that afternoon to have the child removed from the mother's care without knowing the facts. He initiated a life-altering episode for this family and had ripped them apart with no hope of reconciliation or reparation. This so-called therapist caused undue humiliation, embarrassment, and defamation of Melinda to her coworkers and peers by his inaccurate, deceitful, and fabricated allegations based on whatever delusional yarn Stefan spun for the therapist when confronted with the divorce issue. In all the time that he had been seeing that therapist, Stefan had never mentioned or even hinted at there being any negativity associated with his wife or her mothering skills.

A child protective services investigator did come to Melinda's home that evening and opened an investigation of neglect of a child. She was forced to spend tens of thousands of dollars to hire an attorney to defend herself against those gross misrepresentations and otherwise fraudulent allegations. She was trying to protect her son from being taken from her and placed in either foster care with strangers where children are frequently mistreated and/or given minimal care. She was also trying to avoid an even scarier scenario, given to a father who was explosive and abusive. The thought that she needed to defend her livelihood and her ability to support her child in a manner into which he was born and to protect her employment with the state was absolutely revolting. The stress, mental anguish, and financial loss that resulted from Stefan's behavior had been overwhelming!

During the investigations that followed this bizarre incident, it was uncovered that the therapist felt that Stefan had been misdiagnosed and developed a plan for therapy that was contrary to the neurologist's diagnosis. That therapist was not a medical doctor, nor was he any other type of doctor. Therefore, he was not qualified to second-guess the neurologist. He did not know Stefan well enough or long enough to know that his behavior was narcissistic and displayed a victim persona. He should have consulted with the neurologist to develop a plan for therapeutic intervention based on Stefan's explosive personality. The actions of the therapist and the resulting chain of events that followed that evening could have conceivably resulted in someone being seriously injured or killed. Or a beautiful, well-loved baby boy could have been taken from his loving mother and placed either in the custody of the abusive father or placed in foster care.

Whenever I thought of this horrific display of lies and deceit, I could only feel sorry for the monster that Stefan's mother created through her neglect and lies. I was terrified of what Stefan would do next. I no longer wished to help him. I had come to realize that the help that he needed was far beyond my capabilities, and my concerns had now been refocused to Melinda and her child only. Stefan was taken out of the home by child protective services so that the threat of him being close to us had been removed.

However, I spoke to my cousin Jesse, who was a psychologist and was familiar with Stefan because of her employment in that capacity in the town school system where Stefan attended classes. Although she did not interact with Stefan in any professional capacity, we theorized through his interactions with other students and teachers that there was strong evidence of border-line personality disorder, narcissistic personality disorder, as well as sociopathic and psychopathic tendencies. There was not much hope of changing Stefan's behavior or of preventing his abuse and violence, and this would have nothing to do with his closeness or proximity to our property.

Melinda was left with no alternative and filed for divorce. However, Stefan could not deal with this rejection. He called her on a regular basis and told her how much he loved her, how much he missed his child, and was so sweet to her that it was nauseating. My husband and I were very supportive of Melinda and positively reinforced her decision to divorce. However, love was very strange indeed, and I could understand those innate feelings of wanting to make it work out, of not wanting to admit to failure after only one year of marriage. He pleaded with her, begged her, and made all kinds of promises to her. He realized that he wanted his family. He wanted to make his marriage work. There was a laundry list of promises that he made to her as he professed his undying love.

We discouraged her from making a decision that she would live to regret by taking him back. She was reluctant to admit to defeat. She mistakenly believed that if she changed herself, if she did this or that differently, things would get better, and they could have a good marriage. She knew better than this; she was a master's level social worker. She knew better than anyone, but when it came to love and marriage, her heart led her. Logic and thinking and using her intellect had taken a back seat. She was seriously having second thoughts of continuing with the divorce.

Stefan saw that his strategy was working and persisted. He was even bold enough to call me on the telephone and, in his soft, demure, beyond reproach voice, asked, "Mom, hi, it's me,

Stefan. I realize that you are upset with me, but I am calling you for some motherly advice."

In a very curt tone of voice, I asked, "What is it that you want from me?"

He responded, "First of all I would never hurt Melinda or my child. You are a wonderful mother, and I really want to be a part of your family." I personally thought this was bull crap and told him so. He promised to do me proud if he and Melinda got back together. He was so scheming and underhanded that I firmly believed that he was working on a plan to either inflict severe pain or do some other equally harmful and tragic misfortune to us. I was not involved in their marriage, and whatever they worked out between themselves would be their decision, as they were both adults in their late thirties. Whatever resulted from this union would have consequences that would need to be paid for one way or another.

During this very dark period in our lives, the one thing that kept us going was watching that baby grow and develop at an alarming rate. He made us laugh, brought us joy, and knew how to bring smiles to our faces. Around Thanksgiving this little one started waving goodbye to me and his grandfather. He was so darn cute! We loved him so much. At Christmas, his lack of enthusiasm and his inability to understanding the meaning of the season did not deter us from making this holiday as festive as possible for him. We found out that he was very musically inclined. He loved to sing and dance and could even snap his fingers on both hands and delighted in doing so on a regular basis. The child knew that when he did these cute little things, he would elicit a response of positive reinforcement, and he would make us laugh. He was absolutely right in his thinking. That little boy was what gave our lives meaning and made the situation tolerable. Our lives belonged to that precious child.

Right around the holidays of 2006, Melinda and Stefan reconciled. It was not long, however, before the bloom was off the rose. Once he was back in the door, it was just a matter of a month before Stefan once again became abusive and obnoxious with the use of his vulgarities; but worst of all, he now had graduated to physical violence on a regular basis. It broke our hearts to see Melinda covered in bruises. He was very clever in where he attacked her. He never punched her in the face, as then people would see and know what he had done. Rather he would throw objects at her and claim that it slipped from his hand. She had bruises that were so big and colorful that one could feel the pain inflicted just by looking at them.

In February, the month that the Bryce was celebrating his first birthday, we planned a big party at a local restaurant. We thought it was going to be such a happy event, but we really should have known better than that. Stefan made a point of going around to all of Melinda's friends and coworkers and telling them that she was an alcoholic and did drugs and was a terrible mother and any other bad thing that he could think to tell them. Her friends who had known her for years called her and wanted to know what was wrong with her husband. They recounted things that he was saying to them about her, and they were actually afraid for her safety and well-being.

Very shortly after the birthday, Stefan's behavior bizarrely changed. It was very clear to us that there was something awful brewing. We truly believed that he was planning something. You could almost see the calculation going on in his head. He was so preoccupied that he did not have the time or the energy to be abusive during this brief period.

A New Way of Living

2007

Ah, March. Spring was in the air, but today was to be no better than any other day in recent months. Once Melinda had taken care of her family responsibilities, getting Stefan off to work and bathing and feeding the baby, Melinda and I could kick back and have a peaceful cup of coffee and talk for a few minutes. During this time Melinda told me that there had been tension in the air the previous night, and the marital bedroom lacked warmth. Melinda rose early before her husband, in order to avoid any confrontation, so she could send him off to work with a nice lunch, which was also packed with the usual little note telling him she loved him. She put on the coffee for Stefan and slipped back into bed so that he could rise and do his morning routine and be off to work before she would have to get back up and breastfeed the baby. Hopefully she could avoid any unpleasantness.

Stefan got out of bed and began his nervous gyrations, his jerky movements that he does when he does not know quite what to do, and Melinda could tell there was something up—things were not quite right. But what that was she did not know. She lay there in bed and was very uneasy, but she lay very still, and her mind began to wonder as to what could be in store for her on that day. Stefan moved very quickly through the house. She thought that he was grabbing clothing and his lunch container. Suddenly the door slammed, his vehicle started, and he drove away.

Melinda slowly got out of bed as the baby began to whimper. That little boy was hungry and wet, and he would not wait for one minute longer. He was ready to latch on to Mommy and start his day with all the enthusiasm and effervescence of an innocent, young child. His mommy went into his bedroom and greeted her child, and they smiled and cooed at each other as she changed his diaper and readied him for the day's adventures. I came over to share my tea with him and play with him for a few minutes before I had to rush off to work. He enjoyed that interaction every morning. It had been the ritual since he was born, and he looked forward to it.

Once I left, Bryce and Melinda went about their usual daily activities. Mommy made her own baby food, and there was always the never-ending laundry, naptime, cleaning, household chores, and the like. Before she knew it, the day had managed to whisk by, and it was time for daddy to come home.

Stefan's vehicle pulled into the driveway, and he was walking a little funny, as if he had too much beer. He staggered to the top of the stairs and had difficulty opening the door. A short time later, the door opened, and Stefan forcefully entered the apartment. The tension in the air became known immediately upon his entrance. He quickly went into his bedroom and grabbed

Louise Baron-Kent

additional clean clothing out of the closet and the drawers and shoved them into a plastic bag. He went over to where the baby was napping in his swing and grabbed him without benefit of clothing or any consideration that it was his breastfeeding time, screamed at his wife, "I'm taking our child, and I'm never returning." He ran out the door, down the stairs to his vehicle, and threw the baby on the seat and drove off.

Melinda was paralyzed by disbelief and shock. It took her a few moments to internalize and process what was happening. She was overcome with fear for what might happen to her child. She sat on the couch and meditated with her eyes gently closed in an attempt to calm herself and think about where he might go and what he might do and how she might find her child. Melinda was frantic. She made some telephone calls to friends to see if they had seen Stefan. She called family members to query them. Nothing was fruitful.

Once again panic took over, and she was unable to remain calm. She quickly got in her vehicle and drove around to all the places that her husband usually frequented. She drove by the homes of friends, bars, family members, and the like, looking for his vehicle. The more time that passed, the more desperate she became. At long last, she drove by the home of Stefan's sister, and there, hidden in the bushes, she spotted her husband's van. She dashed out of her car to the front door and rang the bell. No one answered. She turned the handle, the door opened, and she walked in. There was Stefan with his sister and the baby on the floor in the living room.

Melinda announced, "I am taking my child, and I am going home." As she attempted to pick up her child, Kathy grabbed her by the hair and pulled her head backward and punched her in the face—breaking her nose. She continued to kick and punch her while Stefan stood there laughing like there was no tomorrow. Melinda begged her husband for some help. All of this transpired in front of her child and Kathy's three young children.

In the meantime, Allen ran upstairs and called their neighbor, Officer Crocquette. She was a captain on the police force, and she would be able to influence a disposal of this situation in their favor. Captain Crocquette was off duty and at her home with her family, across the street from Kathy and Allen's, but rushed right over to take control of the situation. She picked up their telephone and dialed the number to the police station and blurted out, "You need to send four cars immediately to my neighbor's home. We have a life and death situation here, and we need sufficient manpower for physical restraint and arrest." She knew this all prior to her personally assessing the situation.

As Michael and I were about to kick back for a quiet and relaxing evening of television and conversation, my telephone rang. It was approximately seven in the evening, and it was the police department requesting that I come right up to Kathy's house and remove Melinda's vehicle from their property, as Melinda had been arrested for assault. At this point I was so distraught at what had happened that my heart was beating really fast and I could barely breathe. I thought perhaps I was having a heart attack. I was trying to sort things out in my mind and trying to compose myself all at the same time, but all sorts of crazy things were racing through my mind, and the concern for my grandchild was consuming every thought and every movement. As I managed to tell the police that I would be right there and hung up the telephone, my husband had my purse in one hand and the car keys in the other hand. He put his arm around me and said, "We will get through this." We smiled for a brief second at each other and raced out the door.

When we arrived at Kathy's house, there was a chill in the air, and I saw numerous police cars in front, and I thought to myself that they didn't even send out this many police cars when some one had been killed. I thought, *This must be the worst-case scenario—Melinda has killed someone!*

As I got out of my vehicle, with my husband by my side, we went up to the police vehicle parked behind Melinda. I walked up to the first police cruiser I saw and I hastily introduced myself and asked, "What on earth is happening?"

The officer responded in a forthright manner, "Melinda has been arrested for simple assault. She is up at the police station and being processed and will be released in an hour or so."

I said, "I will take my grandchild until she is released."

The officer looked me squarely in the eyes and explained to me, "We are placing custody of the child with the father."

I explained to them, "She is a nursing mother, and you can't place custody of the child with the father without child protective service involvement or some sort of family court intervention."

The officer laughed in my face as he said, "We are the police, and there is nothing that you can do about it. And, if you do not like what is going on and if you persist in resisting us, you will be joining your daughter at the police station."

It was difficult for me to comprehend what they were saying to me. *Resist you?* I was a peaceful and nonviolent person, I was a senior citizen, and I was trying to understand the situation. I was not trying to resist anyone.

For nearly a half hour, I stood in the freezing cold and tried to explain to the police in very simple terms, "There is a pedophile who lives in that house, and they are placing my grandchild in harm's way." My words fell on deaf ears as I tried to explain about the police officer's child that lived across the street being molested by the man that owned that house.

"Surely you could go and speak to her, and she would verify what I am saying to you," I begged. This was all for naught, as the police stood their ground and kept reiterating *ad nauseum* that they were the police and they would not be challenged. This was not making any sense to me. There was protocol that must be followed. Melinda was arrested for trying to protect her child, and the police would make all the decisions. I was consumed with anger, and I needed to find a place to gather my thoughts and compose myself.

Realizing the lateness of the hour and my inability to communicate with these pompous and arrogant police personnel, whom we were taught as young children to respect and to look to for protection, I relented and went home to await the phone call about posting bail.

Shortly after arriving home, the telephone rang, and it was Melinda. She asked me to bring up a certain amount of money for her bail, which we did. However, we could not wait for her as the almighty and omnipotent police told us to go home and await a call as to when we could pick her up. We had no sooner gotten home and they called us to come back and get her. That was a big game that they were playing. Surely it was fun to terrorize people in that manner!

As we were about to leave to pick up Melinda, we saw headlights in the darkness of our driveway, and we peeked out the window. Stefan was dropped off at our house by an unknown vehicle. He came in through the gate and up the stairs to the apartment and unlocked it. He came out a few minutes later and had something tucked under his shirt and held it close to his body. He got in his work van, which was parked in front of our

Louise Baron-Kent

house, and he drove off, all the time looking up at the apartment and smiling, pleased as punch at what he had done.

We did not find out until many months later that the object that he was holding under his shirt was the child's bankbook. Stefan went to the bank and withdrew all of the money that his son had in savings. It was money received from his birth, christening, birthday, and other special occasions. It was all gone and never to be seen again.

As soon as he left, we exited our house and drove to the police station to pick up Melinda. Melinda informed us on the drive home that Stefan came up to the police station and pressed additional charges of larceny. He claimed that Melinda stole the license plates off his work van. When the police questioned her about it, she was ignorant of anything of the sort. However, when they searched her, she had two small screws in her jeans pocket. They were very small and were not the type that would hold a license plate onto a vehicle, and, considering there were two plates on his vehicle and one screw on each side of each plate, it was obvious that these screws were in no way associated to these plates.

In addition, Stefan came to our house while she was being held, and he drove off in his work van, which still had plates on it. When we got home, we sat up talking about the situation late into the evening. There would be no sleeping for us that night. All we could do was re-live the events of the evening and cry. Melinda talked at length with her attorney, who would be at the courthouse first thing the next morning to get a court order to have the child returned.

While Melinda arose early and prepared to go to court, Michael and I drove by his sister's house. We were having an awful rain and windstorm, but we were determined to see his work van. Did it have plates or did it not? We found his Jeep parked at his sister's house and his work van hidden in the bushes of the neighbor's house, and all vehicles had their plates attached. I was armed with my camera, but the weather was so nasty and uncooperative, it was impossible to take any pictures. We did, however, see for ourselves with our own eyes that there were license plates on both vehicles.

Melinda was back from court in record time with the court order for the transfer of the child from the father to the mother forthwith. Stefan's mother refused to relinquish the child, and it was quite obvious that the child was not only traumatized, but he was also terrified. He kept reaching out for me.

We once again had to subject ourselves to the police. They came and removed the child from Erin's arms with her screaming, "I don't want to give this child to that thing!"

What an awful statement to make about your grandson's mother, and in front of him no less. As the police neared closer to me, it was obvious that the child had not slept and cried most of the night. His face was swollen, and his eyes were puffy. He put his arms out to me, and when he was close enough, he grabbed my neck and clung to it and squeezed and squeezed and squeezed and finally fell into a peaceful fitful sleep. He did not move or whimper or eat or have his diaper changed during this entire period. He simply felt safe. He just stayed asleep and resembled an appendage to my neck until early evening. When he finally awoke in the evening, he simply opened his eyes and smiled the sweetest smile anyone could ever imagine from a baby. I felt his love, and he felt mine, and he still did not want to let go and was perfectly content to just sit on me and cuddle. We stayed together as a family, Pappa, Mema, Mommy, and Bryce and just celebrated the well-being and safe return of this baby to its mother until it was time for everyone to go to bed. It was a traumatic experience for all of us, but especially this sweet, innocent baby.

Michael and I talked all night once again about things that Stefan had done previously, things that he continued to do, and we recognized that he would continue to do these awful things and he would make life a living hell, just as he had promised. At this point we had no idea nor could we even conceive of the unbridled evil that was about to be unleashed upon our family.

The next morning, we drove by Kathy's house. His vehicles were still parked in the same spots, but now they had no vehicle tags on them. We were not at all surprised. He wanted Melinda to be punished for something that she had not done. He was an evil and vindictive person. He was very sick! We came home immediately and began helping Melinda pack his belongings and changed the locks so that he could not possibly gain entrance to the building and possibly inflict physical harm to his wife or to his son.

Sometime in the afternoon, the police called my home on two separate occasions to inform us that Stefan would be coming over for his personal belongings. They also called Melinda's house on three separate occasions the same day and requested the same by leaving a message on her answering machine. Each call was answered promptly by me, and I informed them that Melinda had taken her child away to a "safe house" provided by a friend so that they could attempt to get over the trauma they had just experienced without worrying that Stefan might come over and harm them. It was a time to just relax and enjoy each other without all the stress associated with that man. I informed the police of this and told them that they would not return until late Tuesday evening. And they certainly were well aware that she had a court appearance coming up so had no alternative but to return to her home.

I was cleaning up around her apartment and was quite shocked when I found virtually no belongings of his in the apartment. One does not remove all belongings and trappings of life in one fell swoop. This had been planned for some time, and his belongings had been removed piecemeal, but it had gone unnoticed. I informed the police of my findings and told them that if I did find any of his belongings, that I would pack them and bring them to the police station and drop them off.

The very next day, the same ritual began with the police calling Melinda's house and leaving messages and calling my home with regard to his belongings. You would think we were imbeciles or people without brains or something. The number of times they called us amounted to pure harassment! However, I remained cordial, and politely told them the same tale of woe every time they called.

On the day that Melinda returned home with her child, they returned looking well and rested. We spent the evening packing a couple of small boxes of Stefan's personal papers and possessions. When we finished, I called the police to let them know that I would be dropping these boxes off at the police station in the morning. They informed me that they did not want his stuff. But apparently they called him, and he had his friend "Jigger" send Melinda an e-mail requesting that Stefan's belongings be dropped off at Jigger's house and left on his front porch. Michael complied with that request prior to us all going off to court for Melinda's arraignment for the criminal charge of assault.

Because Melinda worked for the state and on the advice of her attorney, she was advised to plead "NOLO Contendre," which is the plea one takes when they throw themselves on the mercy of the courts in exchange for at least consideration of a favorable outcome. It means one is not pleading guilty to any crime, nor are they saying that nothing occurred, but rather leaving it to the courts to listen to the facts and decide if something did in fact happen. Therefore, the charges would be filed for one year, and, providing nothing further happened within that one year period of time, at the end of the period, all charges would be dropped, and she could continue to work in her profession and provide for her family just as if nothing had happened. A no-contact order issued, and Melinda would not be able to have any contact with either Stefan or Kathy.

Just two days later, Stefan went to the courthouse and had the no-contact order dismissed so that he could visit with his son. Melinda did not oppose it, as she really believed in her heart that every child was entitled to see both parents, she being the eternally optimistic social worker and always cognizant of what was in the best interest of the child. The courts made the determination that I, as the maternal grandparent, would facilitate the court's decision of visitation.

Later in the afternoon, an older police officer, identifying himself as Officer Newton, stopped by my house. He announced that he was here so that Stefan could have access to the apartment. I personally thought that the police would have so much more to do with their time than to keep coming to my house demanding access for Stefan. Both Melinda and I recounted the scenario of what happened to Stefan's belongings and that, at his request, were put on the front porch of his friend Jigger's house. Life was becoming unbearable just trying to deal with Stefan and his constant harassment, and now several times daily trying to deal with the police who insisted on access to the apartment.

Melinda had a wonderful friend that she formerly worked with together with her husband and son and who lived in the wilderness. No one except for my husband and I knew how to get to where they lived. They provided a safe haven for Melinda every time she needed a breather. They were a real breath of fresh air in Melinda's life. I suggested, because it had been such a stressful week, that she take her child and visit with her friends for a few days.

On visitation day Erin called me and said, "I will be picking up the child for a visit."

She also had to call Melinda's home and leave a message on her answering machine. I called her back and said, "The court order stated that I, as the maternal grandparent, would facilitate the visit and hand the child over to Stefan."

She insisted, "The court ordered me to work out the visits with her." Apparently she did not know the difference between "maternal" and "paternal" grandparent. I reiterated to her, "If Stefan is not being handed the child, the child will not be going anywhere."

Stefan, Erin, and Jim, came to my house and stood in an angry, defiant line across the street in front of my neighbor's house. Stefan grabbed the baby and immediately announced, "The child has a bruise on his forehead," and handed the child to Erin, who looked at the child and announced, "He has a bruise on his forehead."

Then she handed the child to Jim, and he looked at the child and stated, "He has a bruise on his forehead."

And I thought to myself that these people were idiots, and it gave me some good insight and indication as to how the next eighteen years of visitation would proceed.

Louise Baron-Kent

It was now the middle of March, and Stefan had been stalking us, harassing us, and was being vulgar to us among a whole litany of other juvenile actions, and there was no let up. I truly believed there was something wrong with that man. The house that he owned was diagonally across the street from ours but was on the main thoroughfare. Our home was located on the side street so that our doors were only one hundred fifty feet from each other. He made sure that he was in close proximity to us so that he could impart a regular dose of juvenile bullying.

Life for us was impossible. Because of the close proximity of our dwellings, he always knew what we were doing. Stalking was made very easy for him. Sometimes he lived there, at that house, and sometimes he did not. However, his bullying and other forms of torture were imparted against us in earnest and were daily occurrences. He constantly drove by our house to shout vulgarities at us, throw objects out his vehicle window at us, display his one-fingered salute, follow us, videotape us, photograph us, and whatever else he could think of at the moment that he thought would disturb us.

In all of my years, I have never witnessed another human being, an adult no less, acting in such a juvenile and inappropriate manner. I really dreaded visitation days because I knew that I would have to endure his insane abuse, and I was the one making sure that he got to visit with his child.

On the day after his usual visit, Stefan called me from his cell phone and demanded, "Where is my wife?" He also demanded, "Where is my son?" But that was a secondary question. The real issue was his wife.

I asked him, "Why are you bothering me?"

He yelled at me, "Melinda stays out all night, and I don't like that. I demand that you tell me where she is."

I asked him, "How would you know that? And since you're in the process of getting divorced, why would you care?"

He said, "The neighbors," meaning his friend Jigger in all probability, who lived next door to Stefan, "said you're never home and that you stay out all night."

I told him, "Stefan, that is really none of your concern what she does, and I certainly have no obligation to consult with you about it." I hung up the telephone and called the police, who came and took a report. They promised they would go right over to Stefan's house and tell him to stop bothering me. Within an hour, my doorbell rang. It was Melinda's quasi-friend, Lily. She knew I did not like her, and I let her stand at the door as I asked her, "What is it that you want?"

She informed me, "I received a frantic call from Stefan and really need to talk to you. May I please come in?" The odor of alcohol emanating from her breath was overwhelming. However, I reluctantly indulged her request. Once seated in my living room, she was frantic in her attempt to find out where Melinda and her son were.

"Melinda and her son are safe, and you should know that first hand. You've been at her apartment most of the day visiting with her." I also took advantage of the opportunity to express my feelings that she was no friend of Melinda's by doing this dirty work for Stefan and that now she should leave. She fell down in a drunken episode on her way out the door. The sad reality here was that she was also driving!

When this latest scheme failed, Stefan began calling Melinda's friend Ginger to find out where she was. Stefan had no way of knowing that Ginger was out of town, and the person he was bullying and belittling and being vulgar to on the telephone that day was Ginger's mother, who was very well connected to the state police and the upper echelons of government, who was babysitting while her daughter was away. Once she imparted her words of wisdom on Stefan, he quickly and abruptly hung up the phone.

Life became an all-day adventure whenever Stefan was obsessing. It was overpowering, and it really wore us down. We couldn't let our or her guard down for even a minute, and it really took its toll on everyone. We were constantly staying aware of our surroundings every minute of every day. It became all-consuming trying to protect ourselves.

Several days later we had to be present at the courthouse once again for the continuation hearing of Stefan, in order for him to get the criminal restraining order against him dismissed so that he could continue visiting with his child. He presented himself to the judge to be the kindest, most caring, and thoughtful individual who ever walked the face of this earth, and you could actually see that butter melting in his mouth. However, nothing could have been farther from the truth—the real Stefan.

The snow had been falling all day and continued after we left the courthouse and arrived home. Stefan and his friend Jigger showed up out of the blue and, without asking, began to shovel snow from my driveway.

Michael arrived home from work and when he noticed them in our yard, he was furious. "You stalk us, harass us, and bully us, and now you're in my yard shoveling snow? I don't think so! We don't need the likes of you here doing what I could do perfectly well myself."

Stefan shouted vulgarities and obscenities at Michael and came very close to punching him but instead attacked his manhood verbally because Michael did not fight and argue about every little thing like Stefan did. That would have been a big mistake to physically attack Michael, as he was three times his size and a senior citizen.

On Tuesday, March 20, Stefan's visitation day, he did not call. He and his friend Jigger walked over and stood in front of my neighbor's yard across the street. I saw them coming from the window and readied the baby and brought him down to his father. When Stefan returned the child at six forty p.m., the baby got a little fussy, and Stefan kissed him and said to him, "Don't worry, honey. This is only temporary." He handed me the baby, and I kissed him, and as I did so, Stefan said to the baby, "Keep kissing Grandma, 'cause it's all coming to an end soon!"

I had no idea what he meant by that remark, but we hustled into the house where it was cozy and warm. It was the same scenario for the visitation two days later, except that along with the verbal abuse, there were, of course, his signature hand gestures.

Five days later, we learned what Stefan's comments meant. Stefan had filed another complaint of neglect with the child protective services. Not that there was any neglect or mistreatment, but rather to get even with Melinda and embarrass her once again. Now, quite satisfied with what he had done, there were no confrontations at the next several visits. He was very smug and thought he was in complete control.

On the last day of the month, we went out for our usual Friday baby bonding adventure. We took him for a walk in the park. When we arrived home, we came straight to my house so that we could hang out and play with Bryce and his toys. Melinda went to her house to get some books so we could read to the baby. She no sooner left my home than I heard a loud thud. As I ran to the door to see what it was, I saw Melinda standing there, crying. Her face was very red, and a case of diapers lay on the ground. Stefan came by and threw these at her, striking her in the face. She called the police, and Stefan was arrested for assault and another no-contact order was issued.

Now that there was a new no-contact order in effect, it affected Stefan's visit with his child on Easter Sunday, and there was no way of arranging that visit with the order in place. Jigger came to my door and rang my bell and inquired, "Will there be a visit today?"

I informed Jigger, "I do not know anything."

Jigger was polite, although intoxicated at this early hour of Easter Sunday, and he said, "I will pass this along to Stefan."

Jigger got into Stefan's van, and they sat outside our house stalking us all day. When Michael and I left in our truck, Stefan made his usual obscene gestures toward us.

Once again, after several court appearances and continuances, we were back in court for the trial of Melinda emanating out of Kathy's complaint of assault. The whole family was present—Kathy, Erin, and Jim. Melinda was also being tried on the new charge of larceny of Stefan's license plates. After all was said and done, the prosecutor refused to prosecute the charge of larceny, stating that it was ridiculous and there was no proof. Therefore, those charges were dropped, and it angered Stefan. When the family left the courthouse, Stefan, knowing we were watching at the window until we could see that they were driving away, checked out his mother and sister to make sure they were not looking and twice looked up and blew Melinda kisses and mouthed, "I love you!" I wanted to vomit.

During a civil moment during our numerous court appearances and continuances, Stefan's mother and I worked out an arrangement for the facilitation of visitation with Bryce. She would pick up Bryce at my home and drop him off there when the visit was finished. On the very first visitation day, she called Michael and said she would pick up the child at five p.m. She did not arrive until five thirty p.m. When she finally arrived, I said, "You know, if this arrangement is going to work—and I am not saying this out of anger, but rather out of fundamental fairness—a certain time means a certain time."

We spoke cordially to each other for a few seconds about personal issues, and she left with the child. When she returned the baby, she rang my doorbell and we exchanged a few pleasantries, and, as she was leaving, she asked me, "Can this be the new Tuesday/Thursday ritual for visitation?"

I said, "That would be fine."

Every time things sort of smoothed out and I had a sense that everything was going to be all right, someone in the family would start slinging the mud. They would lure us into this false sense of security, and then *bam!*

Although Kathy had a no-contact order in effect, she also felt she needed a restraining order against Melinda. Once again, we were back in court. Kathy showed up in court without an attorney, and the case was continued for three weeks to give her ample time to obtain one. She obtained the services of an attorney from legal services, stating that she was indigent, even though she ran a daycare; and she and her husband jointly owned a successful grocery store. These people had no use for truth. Every word that came out of their mouths was for convenience, persuasion, and manipulation of fact.

On the next visitation day, Melinda called me and asked me to come and look at Bryce. She thought he felt quite hot and needed a grandmotherly opinion. I hurried over with thermometer in hand and took the temperature of Bryce. It was high enough to place a call to the pediatrician, who ordered bed rest for him and if not better with a few hours a visit to the doctor's office was recommended. I called Erin and informed her, "The baby has been sick with a fever. A visit is tentative at this point in time." She called me several times and asked, "How is he feeling?" And, shortly before the pick-up time, she called and demanded a visit. "I do not want Stefan to be disappointed," she confessed. She proceeded to tell me, "Melinda has been calling Stefan all day, telling him there will be no visit."

I interrupted her right there and said, "I am not going there. Melinda and Stefan are adults, and I am not interested in what they have to say to each other. My only concern is for the child, and neither you nor Stefan are going to bully me into putting that child's health at risk and more especially to alleviate Stefan's personal disappointment and anger."

It was now Stefan's turn to try to coerce and bully me into letting him have a visit with Bryce. He never asked how the child was doing; he just insisted on having his visit. As always, it was all about Stefan.

Bryce was not doing better in a few hours, and he had developed a bright red rash all over his body. Melinda and I ended up taking him in for an emergency visit. The doctor's orders were for no further visitation until he cleared Bryce for visits. I telephoned Erin and advised her of the doctor's decision.

After a day and a half of bed rest and some tender loving care from Mom, Bryce was looking so much better and feeling so much better, and a call to the doctor cleared the way for him to have a visit with his father on Sunday.

Stefan, however, always had to push the envelope. He called me on Saturday and asked if he could also see the child on Saturday, as he wanted to take him to a birthday party. The message was relayed to Melinda, who immediately made arrangements for the child to be picked up for the party.

On Sunday Stefan picked up the child at ten thirty in the morning and was to have him back home at two thirty in the afternoon. Michael and I spent the day working around the yard. It was the end of April, and the day was a gift from heaven—sunny and warm. It was a perfect day for yard work and enjoying nature. We were just walking back up the street from emptying the wheelbarrow of yard debris down the railroad banking, when I noticed Stefan standing in front of my neighbor's house. When I reached him he handed me a bag of clothes that were dirty. He told me the child had on new clothing received as a Christmas present and that he had gotten the child a haircut. But when I reached for the baby, he would not relinquish him and said, "Do not to touch him. You are dirty."

I said, "Stop it. Who do you think you are?" and I grabbed the child from him. As I was walking across the street, he came running over and "ripped" the hat the child was wearing off of his head and yelled, "I will give it back to him when the child comes to live with me forever!" I shook my head in disbelief and just kept on walking.

The next day we had to be in court for Stefan's assault charges. We spent several hours there, and the case was continued to May 14. As soon as Stefan saw us walk in, he ran over to us and started jumping up and down, waving his fists in our faces, yelling that I was a liar and that Melinda was a liar, only the expletives of the type of liar that we were would make one's hair curl. He needed to be redirected by his stepfather, Jim. Jim then proceeded to sit in the courtroom, got Melinda's attention, and made the loser symbol on his forehead with his fingers and pointed at Melinda.

After watching this juvenile, inappropriate behavior from two grown men for several hours, I called Erin on her cell phone and informed her, "I will no longer participate in the arrangement we worked out to facilitate the visits for Stefan and Bryce, and I will no longer subject myself to their barbarism."

For the next several months Michael, Melinda, and I tried heroically to respect every family member on both sides of this acrimonious divorce and to always remain cognizant of the needs of the child first and foremost. It was truly a sad day when adults acted like buffoons and so delighted in the playing out of these adolescent absurdities for their own personal edification, rather than being committed to the safety and well-being of such a delightful child.

The Annihilation
Commences

2007

Once again, Melinda filed for divorce. She was firm in her convictions that this was a necessary evil. She had to think of her child first. We, as parents, would give her and her son all the love and support that we could possibly give them, and we would all weather that storm together. That too would pass.

Officer Crocquette, Kathy's neighbor who was a captain on the police force, recommended an attorney for Stefan. She told him that he must retain Skip Baldini. He was not a particularly good attorney, but he was well connected and loyal to his clients. His father, Arthur Baldini, was the former police chief, and Skip rode on his father's coattails. Skip was appointed as the town magistrate as a perk to his father. Since the father passed away from all the stresses associated with defending himself in a scandal at another police department at which he worked, Skip took over the role of being the unofficial head of the police department since becoming appointed town magistrate. To put it bluntly, he had great influence over police personnel, and no one dared violate that code of conduct.

I remember Skip as being a lifelong resident of our town who had become a mediocre zoning attorney. He attempted to push through an unfavorable zoning variance in my neighborhood, and the neighbors were up in arms. It did not directly affect me because I was not within the radius of notification, but I saw that my neighbors were having great difficulty in defeating the variance. Being familiar with zoning issues somewhat and having a solid background in law, I offered to help them get organized and fight to win. They gladly accepted my help. After numerous scheduled meetings and postponements because of the attorney's violations of zoning law procedures, endless research of various laws of the town, unending investigation, and interminable communications between neighbors and outside agencies, the zoning hearing was finally held. We, being neighbors and now friends, walked out of that meeting victorious. Neighbors were thankful for my help and dedication to the neighborhood, and Skip was asking my son-in-law, Stefan, "Who was that woman?" Now that he was representing Stefan in the divorce proceedings, he had a personal vendetta against me.

Just by the very fact that Mr. Baldini was the municipal judge in our town should have disqualified him from representing Stefan in the divorce proceedings as a conflict of interest. And then coupled with the fact that Attorney Baldini was just bested by me in a zoning issue should have sent up a red flag that clearly there was a conflict going on here. But wait, it got even better. Skip Baldini was married to Babs Baldini. Babs was also an attorney at the attorney general's office. She had worked there for many years and was now up into the supervisory ranks. She would be the person who would push through and prosecute Melinda over and over again without probable cause or evidence in order to help her husband to help his client. For them it was a win-win situation! Baldini controlled and directed police personnel and controlled the attorney general for ease of prosecution and pleased his client and gave him *carte blanche* to further control and abuse his wife. The term for this had now become coined into the phrase "domestic violence by proxy."

From that point forward, our lives consisted of boundless invasions of our home by the police department, albeit precipitated by calls from Stefan when he was obsessing about his soon-to-be former wife. Stefan would call the police and report that she was being neglectful of their child by being drunk or strung out on drugs, and the police would come to my home late in the evening and bang on my windows with their batons until we were awakened. As we answered the door, they forcefully yelled, "Where is Melinda?"

"You know that she does not live here, so why do you keep coming to my house to look for her?" They would leave my house and immediately go next door and bang on Melinda's door until she was awakened and began questioning her about how much she had to drink, and what kind of drugs she was taking, etc.

Every night the answer was the same. She was in her own home, she had not had anything to drink, she did not do drugs, and she was in bed sleeping, and there were no men there. However, they always made a point to go into her house and search. They never did find a thing and clearly did not have any authority or probable cause to enter or search her apartment. Nor did they ever ask for any type of blood test or drug testing. They did not follow protocol and acted in a personal capacity because Stefan requested it. Clearly, it was a violation of her civil rights.

One night when Stefan was over the top in his obsessing, he called the police and told them something so bizarre that they sent twelve police vehicles, two fire trucks, and two rescue trucks. The blaring of the sirens and the flashing of the lights on the vehicles was enough to bring out many of the neighbors into the streets. No one had any idea what was happening. We all thought surely with all of the police personnel and medical personnel and all of the vehicles and trucks, someone must have been murdered at the least.

When I approached the police personnel in charge and inquired, "What is going on here?" They, of course, would tell me nothing, but it did all boil down to Stefan. After hours of standing out in the cold trying to figure out what on earth was going on, I asked the police, "Is there any crime that has been committed by anyone here on my property?" They responded in the negative. I then said, "If no crime has been committed and there is no reason for you to be here, then get off my property!"

The police informed me, "You are not safe here with your daughter." Laughter just welled up in my being as I told them, "You are right. I am not safe. But it is because of that man standing on the corner just jubilating and gyrating in the darkness that I am not safe—he scares the hell out of me." Stefan—he was the one who made everyone in our neighborhood unsafe.

By the time all of the police vehicles, fire apparatus, and rescue trucks vacated my premises, it was the wee hours of the morning and another night without sleep. For hours, this nonsense continued. It must have been a really slow night for the police department to deploy so much in the way of precious resources. So much so, that the taxpayers would now pay dearly for this evening's obsessions of Stefan.

Every time the police were dispatched to my property, there was Stefan, standing on the corner, jubilating and gyrating in excitement. One would think the police would have better things to do with their time and taxpayers' money. The police were visiting with us at least once a week for months and occasionally two or three times a week. Being jolted out of bed in the middle of the night became a way of life for us, and it was taking its toll on our physical well-being.

And so life went on in this uncivilized fashion for our family. We tried to stay focused on Bryce and give him the best life that he possibly could have under the circumstances. This child was the joy that held us all together. We thank God every day for him. His laughter was what made us laugh; his being gave all of us a reason for being, and his innocence made us very aware and determined that we all must be his voice until he was old enough and had enough maturity to speak out for himself.

We spent most of our days being in family court for the divorce proceedings and/or dealing with the police. It was not a life; it was more of an existence. Stefan stalked us regularly; he was constantly taking pictures of us, calling us, harassing us, and did whatever he could to make our lives not worth living. We had called the police on numerous occasions, and they did nothing to help us. Their response to us was that "we" must learn not to anger Stefan. "We" must learn how to follow the rules. "We" must learn how to get along! So police protection for us was a dead-end street. They did not want to hear anything we had to say.

Michael and I were both born and raised in that town and led exemplary lives there. We had lived in the same house and neighborhood for over forty years. Helping our neighbors was something we enjoyed and did gladly. There had never been any negative involvement with the police or neighbors. We lived in a wonderful community, and we delighted in a peaceful existence. But now, our lives in our golden years evolved into learning how to live with the police coming to our doors just about every visitation day, because Stefan had called them with some obsessive, bizarre, fabricated story.

That kept the police very, very busy, as we lived in a neighborhood of congested multi-family dwellings. People did not think anything of parking in front of someone else's house, as long as they had someplace to park. That kept Stefan's imagination in overdrive. On one occasion, my sister-in-law stopped by our house on a cold, drizzly January morning so that Michael could check her tires. Stefan came running right out of his house with his camera in hand, taking pictures and, before long, the police arrived. He must have sat in his window with binoculars watching our house in order to know when a new car had shown up. There was something very sick going on here.

There was no end to his laundry list of evil deeds that he would do to make our lives unbearable. He would have either his mother or girlfriend call the gas and electric companies and have the services turned off, stating that the residents had moved. When the utility companies came to the property to turn off the specific utility, there was Stefan in his yard, jubilating and gyrating and jumping in excitement and laughing.

When I called the service providers, they said, "Yes, a female called to have the services discontinued."

I informed them, "I am the owner of the property, and nothing has changed. You need to reconnect the utility immediately."

Stefan did not care that his son would have no heat or hot water. All he cared about was getting even with his wife, as he was ordered to pay for these services by the judge of the family court, and he deemed that inappropriate. He was also ordered to pay all of the household expenses for his wife and son. But no one was going to order him to pay for anything.

The police took over as the aggressors when Stefan was not able to do it himself in person. They began watching our house, and it was an all-out attack. Neighbors would call to warn us where the police were parked and whether they had binoculars and for how long they knew them to be watching. It was as if there was a conspiracy of some sort. It was absolutely unbelievable. What had we ever done to anyone to deserve this? Things like this did not happen here. We were in America, and we had civil rights and constitutional rights. But how could we enforce those rights when the police were involved in the violation of them? We constantly had to stay one step ahead of Stefan, or we had to do damage control after his obsessive episodes. It had become a full-time job staying one step ahead of the game. It was sometimes difficult to figure out who the real enemy was— Stefan, his family, the police, Skip Baldini? Or perhaps even all of them.

On a warm day in May, we had to be in court again because of Kathy and her infamous restraining orders and—once again, true to form—we sat there most of the day and finally the matter got continued. Kathy had presented by herself, and when we were leaving, I smiled at her and we went our separate ways. While picking up the child from a visit with his father, Stefan sat outside of the police station, parked in his Jeep with the child sitting in the vehicle with him. When I arrived, I went directly into the police station, which I usually did to keep from exposing myself to Stefan's verbal attacks when the exchange took place outside of the police station. Stefan finally walked into the station and handed me the child. Stefan left without attack, and while the child was saying goodbye to the police officer, Stefan came storming back in and excitedly started yelling, "I want to file a complaint against that woman. She called my family baboons in court today." He went on and on about what a bad person I was, that I was no good, I was ridiculous, and all while I was standing there holding his child. The officer motioned for me to leave and he would handle Stefan. Stefan was not even in court that day, so this episode was just something that he had been obsessing about.

With each visit came new attacks and accusations, and I would ask myself, *Why am I doing this to myself?* It got to the point that it became a tremendous strain on me. Sleep was evasive. I went to work morning after morning with eyes red and swollen from lack of sleep. Functioning in an intelligent manner and earning a living became increasingly difficult. But I endured, not for me, but for the love of my grandchild. I did it because I did not want Melinda to get involved in a hostile situation by having to go near him. She had to deal with enough as it was.

On a particular Friday in September, with the days of summer waning and fall fast approaching, we decided to take Bryce out to lunch at a friend's café and have some fish and chips and play a few games of Keno and then go to the park. He was getting so big. He really enjoyed going speedily down the slide and ending in the safety of my arms at the bottom. He would laugh and laugh and want to do it all over again. His mom would climb to the top with him and let him go, and I never failed to be there for him; he always landed safely in my arms.

It had been an all-day adventure. We left the house around eleven thirty a.m. and went to the Full House Café. Bryce liked to wander around talking to the patrons and playing pinball. He, of course, was too small to actually play pinball, but I would put a chair in front of me, and we would play together. He would get so excited with all the bright lights and noises that the machine made. Our fish and chips came, and we all sat down to lunch and enjoyed our conversation and watched the activities and other patrons interacting with our little one. After lunch, we sat around talking and playing Keno while Bryce was finishing up his food.

Fridays were always our special bonding day. It was a real plus for all of us. At about a quarter to two, we headed out and drove over to the park for an hour of play and doing my favorite—taking pictures of a little boy enjoying his afternoon at the park with his family. We arrived home shortly after three p.m. As we approached the house, standing in our driveway was a friend of Melinda's whom she had not seen in years. We were so surprised to see him after all this time. He was driving a motorcycle, and Bryce's eyes lit up when he saw it. He sat on it as we held him, and we visited outside for about a half hour with the friend. The friend left, and we all headed to the apartment for naptime. It was a wonderful day. It was always good when we could get away and not have do deal with the evils of the world.

About a week or so later, the police arrived at Melinda's house and placed her under arrest for violation of a protective order. It had occurred to us that Kathy now had a restraining order against Melinda. We had all endured direct attacks from Stefan. However, he was not successful in getting Melinda incarcerated. Then we endured the tyrannical actions of the police, and, even with all of their intervention and surveillance, there were never any probable causes for arrest. So now we had moved into the next phase of torture—enter Kathy with her restraining orders.

Kathy's claim was that, on that particular Friday, we were participating in our usual Friday bonding outing, Melinda drove her vehicle past her husband's house, saw Kathy standing outside, rolled down her vehicle's driver's side window, and yelled vulgarities at Kathy, and that this occurred at twelve thirty p.m. on that day.

How could this be possible? We were not even home. Because of all of the vandalism that Stefan had done to our property, we had video surveillance cameras installed so that we could view the property from any angle at any given time and record any activity. In addition, we had the pictures from the park and the technology of the modern digital camera records the time and date on the pictures. What an invention! We told this to the police at the time of arrest, and their response was to "tell it to the judge." They did not want to hear anything. It was always so much more fun for them to rip her child from her arms, place her in handcuffs, and drag her off to the police station for arraignment.

In the beginning of October, we were back at court for Melinda's trial on the violation charge. We were armed with the video surveillance tape, which was date and time stamped, that showed us leaving my residence in my vehicle at approximately eleven thirty a.m., making a left turn to head in the opposite direction of Stefan's house, and arriving back at my premises around three p.m. It also showed that Melinda's vehicle never moved from the driveway that day.

The person who owned the restaurant where we had lunch also testified that we were at his place that day for several hours. And the pictures of our precious baby having fun at the park were date and time stamped for that afternoon. The judge found Melinda not guilty, citing overwhelming evidence that the incident never happened. Kathy and her brother were furious. We heard the prosecutor telling Kathy to keep trying—sooner or later something would stick. I guess it was pretty easy to do if her attorney controlled the police personnel and the attorney's wife worked in a supervisory capacity at the attorney general's office—piece of cake.

After this incident, I began keeping a diary on a daily basis just so that I could look back on any particular day to refresh our memories of where we were, what we were doing, and dates and times. Stefan's family was fast and furious in their attempts to have Melinda taken care of for once and for all. It made my head spin. It was overwhelming, and I wanted to scream. Normal people did not behave in that manner.

We were barely out of the courthouse when Stefan went to the police station to file a new complaint that his wife committed trespass against him. Yikes! How on earth did she do this? This was his wife, the mother of his child. Trespass? How did someone do this to his wife? The police again arrived at our home and arrested Melinda for trespassing. There was nothing to offer in Melinda's defense. She could go to prison for some indefinable crime that she did not commit. Once again, Melinda was arraigned at the courthouse and became a part of the criminal process.

When Melinda was called, the judge was just as belligerent as he was on the previous two occasions. He ordered bail in the amount of two thousand dollars. *Two thousand dollars?* I was thinking to myself. The alleged crime was trespassing—not bank robbery or rape! Melinda's lawyer told the judge, "She has one thousand with her. Would you consider that in light of the pettiness of the crime?"

He barked back from behind a face red and blemished from many years of alcohol abuse, "Tell her to show me another thousand," as he snickered.

I sat there quietly and tears ran down my face, my body shaking uncontrollably in disbelief as the handcuffs clicked shut around Melinda's wrists, and she was pulled away like a sack of rotting potatoes to the holding cell until I could come up with the remainder of the bail.

I had never witnessed anything like this before in my life. We were not criminals. We were educated, productive members of society. How could that be happening? I was paralyzed by fear for my child, and the sound of the handcuffs closing kept replaying in my head. I could not move and did not even realize that I was crying so hard that an elderly gentleman dressed in a suit sitting behind me had put his arm around me to console me. I could no longer even see the people in the courtroom. All I could hear was the clicking of those damn cuffs.

After sitting quietly for a brief period of time and calming myself, I was able to get up and out of the courthouse. I now had to run all over town trying to come up with the remainder of the bail money. My checking account didn't allow for such large amounts in a cash withdrawal, and there was no possibility of getting to my bank in a timely fashion to make a personal withdrawal at this hour, so I had to come up with another way to get that money. I went to several banks trying to get a cash advance on my American Express card, but banks in the city no longer offered that service. It took me the remainder of the day to produce that amount of money. However, I managed it through the intermittent tears and sobbing and went back to the courthouse to free my child. I prayed that no other mother would have to live through seeing her child treated in the manner in which my daughter was treated.

On the day of the trial, the prosecutor offered a plea deal. He wanted Melinda to plead guilty to trespass and receive a light sentence. I was enraged.

She had not done anything. The prosecutor offered as his only evidence, a cell phone picture of the back of some person dressed in a sweatshirt with a hood on it. No one could really tell whether this person was male or female. It had no date or time stamp, and no one could determine where the picture was taken. When Stefan took the stand he contradicted everything that the police officers so fortuitously set up for the prosecutor through their testimony, and the judge dismissed the case. Once again Stefan was beside himself. He immediately went to the police department and filed a new complaint of assault.

I was in disbelief that there was no let up in his persistence to have Melinda incarcerated. Melinda had gone from being a productive member of society to a criminal with an arrest record longer than a roll of toilet paper. How did that happen?

When the family returned the child from a visit with Stefan, Erin handed the child to Michael, who was reaching out to the child and saying, "You want to come and see Pappa?"

Erin put on her plastic smile and called to Michael in an ever so ooey-gooey manner like she was his new best friend. Michael ignored her, as he always did. She looked at me and said, "What does he call you two?"

I replied, "What does it matter to you? Just make something up. You are all really good at that!"

Stefan went into an explosive fit and started yelling and gyrating and screaming, "You will see how much I can make up. You just wait!"

One night in the middle of November, around ten o'clock, I was awakened by the pounding on my front door. It was the police who, demanded to know where Melinda might be. There were at least three police officers and two police cars. I informed them, "You just awakened me from a sound sleep."

They insinuated, "You must be hiding her in your house, because we cannot find her?" I did not know what they were even talking about, as I was sleeping and had been asleep since seven thirty p.m. because I was not feeling well. They asked me, "Is she home?"

I responded, "I don't know. I was asleep."

They then proceeded to ask me, "Where is her car?"

Once again I responded, "I do not know. I was asleep."

They kept up the interrogation and badgering and wanted to know what vehicle she was driving. As I looked out into the driveway, I could see that Melinda's vehicle was in the driveway.

They told me, "We pounded on her door and there was no answer."

I told them, "Just because her car is here in the driveway it is not an indication of whether or not she is home. Her friend picked her up on Friday evening to spend the weekend with her, as she frequently does. But, because I had been sleeping, I did not know whether or not she had returned yet."

After the police left, I entered Melinda's apartment and found that she was not there. I called her on her cell phone, and there was no answer, and then I was worried. Michael and I drove to the safe house and found them all asleep, and we were relieved.

About a week later the police arrived at my home and arrested Melinda for the assault charge. And unbeknownst to us, Stefan's mother had been working diligently behind the scenes, calling Melinda's place of employment in an attempt to get her fired. Here she was trying to make small talk with us to find out information about what the child called us, and she was calling Melinda's employer on a regular basis to complain about her and have her employment terminated. However, we needed to address what was at hand. We needed to concentrate and stay focused.

Melinda was arraigned in the afternoon for the assault charge. It was the very same judge who did all of the arraignments, and I expected a repeat performance of the previous arrest. It was after lunch, and the judge's face glowed a rosy red as he ordered personal recognizance instead of bail. I was stunned by his announcement. Apparently the justice that was meted out after lunch was a lot less severe than the justice meted out before lunch. That was truly a strange form of justice. That was our justice system at its finest. There was no rhyme or reason to it. Hit or miss justice was what I called it.

Trial day arrived in November, and Stefan took the stand and told the judge how Melinda came to his house around seven o'clock one evening and assaulted him. She had punched him in the head and told the judge that it occurred on the last weekend in October. Once again, Stefan was unaware that Melinda spent her weekends at a "safe house" far away. The owner of that home testified in Melinda's behalf and stated that she was present at the home all weekend long, together with her husband, and at no time did Melinda leave that home. The friend drove her home in her own vehicle together with her child on Wednesday afternoon. After a preponderance of the evidence, Melinda was found not guilty.

In between all of that criminal activity, there was also the matter of the divorce, visitation, custody issues, and the like. We spent endless hours in the family court. There was testimony from Stefan and his family about how awful we all were and how wonderful they all were. The judge was not happy with Stefan's behavior, and numerous hearings were scheduled and rescheduled because of Stefan's actions. We attended and held our heads up high. We stared at the family and wondered how they could do all they had done to a small child because they hated his mother. Hate was a very strong word. But their feelings for Melinda went beyond hate, and I had a hard time understanding how people could behave like that.

We did, however, pick up some useful information from those hearings. We discovered that Stefan had a girlfriend, and had one for some time, but we did not know who she was or what she looked like. She must have been a very desperate woman.

During the Thanksgiving Day festivities at my home, Stefan and Kathy showed up at my home, knowing they had no-contact and restraining orders against Melinda. Knowing that Melinda was in her own home and had nowhere to go to protect herself, they rang my doorbell to pick up Bryce for a holiday visit and cause a scene. Kathy decided to give another shot at incarcerating her sister-in-law. They stopped at the police department the very next day and filed charges of violating a no-contact order.

Melinda was once again arrested, and her trial was held a few days before Christmas. She was terrified that she would be incarcerated and would not be able to see her child on Christmas day. Her attorney advised that the case could go either way. There were no guarantees of how the judge would view the situation. He again advised her to plead "NOLO." Not wanting to take the chance of being away from her son or her family for the holidays, she took the plea and was given one-year probation for a sentence. She was released and spent Christmas with her child. The judge made note of Melinda's criminal record and expressly stated that he was sick of it all and gave us some indication that if she had not taken the plea, he would have incarcerated her for the holidays and taken her away from her young child!

Thus far, neither Stefan, his mother, nor his sister, had been successful in incarcerating Melinda in order to bolster their position in the family court hearings for obtaining sole custody of the child. That, of course, was the ultimate plan. If the mother was in prison, it was considered abandonment of her child. It would be irrelevant that the father, girlfriend, and/or other family member fabricated a story in order for that incarceration to occur.

We endured our daily dose of bullying from Stefan and his stalking and his violence against our daughter and her child. There was truly no help for us. When something happened, we did not even bother to call the police any longer. We had learned to endure. Someday, someone would die, and it would be over, and we would have fallen through the cracks, and the police would claim that they did not know. That was all that we had to look toward.

It was the Christmas season, and I had no spirit left in me. I had been worn down, and I could only imagine how Melinda was feeling. There was no desire on my part to shop for Christmas, and there was no desire to be with my family or friends at this special time of year. It was very hard just to get up each morning and function as a rational human being. I did not sleep, I could not eat, and I did not care anymore. I was running on empty. I could not go on with all of that abuse. I would not be put in fear of my life so that Stefan could have a visit with his child.

One morning I got out of bed and went directly to the court-house to obtain a restraining order against Stefan. It took me all day to get that restraining order. The judge treated me one step lower than the scum on the bottom of someone's shoe because Mr. Baldini represented Stefan. I would not be allowed a restraining order until the magistrate spoke with Mr. Baldini, and he agreed to allow it.

What was this world coming to? Mr. Baldini had to allow for me to have a restraining order? Yeah, fat chance of that happening. When I went back before the judge in the afternoon in front of Mr. Baldini, to my surprise, a temporary order was granted to me. Apparently, Mr. Baldini read Stefan the riot act, and it was the most relaxing weekend that I have had in a long time. We remained ever vigilant, and I could not help but think that this was nothing more than the calm before the storm.

On Sunday evening we were up and down all night. It was so peaceful and quiet, that it scared us. We were supposed to be in court for the hearing on my restraining order right after the Christmas holiday; however, there was a death in my family, and I called the court to have it continued, and they were agreeable. I tried to get help from legal services, but they could not help me because they represented Kathy in her restraining orders, and that would be a conflict of interest. After the hundreds of thousands of dollars that we had spent in helping Melinda, I could not afford to pay for an attorney to obtain this restraining order, so I thought it best to represent myself and take my chances.

My wish for this Christmas holiday could not be bought. It would cost nothing. I prayed for a Christmas miracle. My wish was that somehow Stefan would transform into a human being and conduct himself in a civilized manner so that things could get better. I believed and wanted it so badly, but it never happened. When my brother-in-law said grace before the Christmas dinner, I asked him to kick in a little something extra for having a better New Year than we had in 2007.

We arrived at court for the hearing on my restraining order. I had my witnesses with me. They remained in the courtroom when I got up to go to the ladies' room. On the way back into the courtroom, Stefan and his stepfather were outside in the hallway sitting on a table. Suddenly, Stefan popped up from his perch on the table and started toward me saying, "There she is, you fu—"

Jim grabbed him by the collar and stopped him. I reported it to court personnel, who did nothing. The matter was continued once again, as I was without benefit of an attorney. The judge chastised me, saying that this would be the last continuance. I was in complete agreement. The temporary restraining order remained in effect until it was either dismissed at hearing or continued after hearing. In either case, the police department received a copy of the order for their records.

While picking up our grandchild at the police station after a visit one Sunday in January, Stefan carried the child into the station, and Michael went in after him. Michael walked out carrying the child, and Stefan was immediately behind him, heckling him and trying to goad him into doing something. Michael ignored him and kept walking. Stefan became enraged that Michael ignored him. He pulled out his camera phone, started taking pictures of Michael, and walked right over to my vehicle and started taking pictures of me. He yelled loudly that his wife was sleeping with his best friend. I turned off my vehicle's engine and went into the police station and rang the bell to speak to the officer on desk duty. I told him, "I have a restraining order, and I am not supposed to be harassed."

The officer promptly informed me, "The station is neutral ground, and Stefan can do whatever he likes."

I quickly came to the realization that even a restraining order would not protect me. The restraining order meant nothing.

The appointed day finally arrived for the restraining order hearing. I was apprehensive because I did not have an attorney. Once again, I would be up against Attorney Baldini. My cousin, my husband, and my sister-in-law all came to testify for me. The judge made note of Stefan's mother, who was sitting in the front row. She asked her, "Please move to the back of the room, as I do not want to look at you. Your facial expressions are making me ill." Erin complied, but when the judge looked up again she stated, "I can still see your stupid expressions, and if you can't find a place in the courtroom where I can't see your face, you can leave." Once again she complied. The hearing went surprisingly well and the judge granted the restraining order for six months. Hopefully, the divorce would be final within that period of time, and I would not need it any longer.

Life was still going on all around us, but our participation was minimal. We had lost contact with friends and family. We did not go anywhere. We did not do anything. It was all that we could do to keep on going.

The Annihilation
Intensifies

Everyone in our family was suffering from post-traumatic stress disorder, was treated by physicians, and on medication to help lessen the anxiety associated with the disorder and the sleep deprivation. We would hear a police siren, and we would be terrified and instantly relive all the abuse that we had suffered thus far from the police. We would see a police vehicle, and we would immediately go in a different direction and attempt to minimize our existence. The terror that we felt was palpable, and it was almost more than we could bear.

Life became so unbearable. We endured Stefan's wrath every visitation day. The surprising part was that both Erin and Jim, at most times, acted just as juvenile in their behavior as Stefan did. He not only bullied us, but he also bullied the daycare mother as well. Anyone associated with his child or our family were fair game for his indignations. There was never a time when there was breathing room where we could just relax and say everything was all right. It was important to stay vigilant and prepared. Expect the unexpected. Never let our guard down.

My neighbor called me one morning and said, "Stefan is out in my driveway taking pictures of your house. I am so sick and tired of him jumping my fence and perching in my yard in order for him so see what is going on at your house."

After I hung up the telephone from our conversation and went outside a few minutes later to empty my trash, Stefan was still there stalking us and taking pictures. I had a restraining order against him for preventing him from doing this sort of behavior, and I called the police and filed a report. Officer Newton, who was a friend of Stefan's, was dispatched and took a report and talked to my neighbor, who told the officer, "he does this constantly, and I am afraid of him. Something needs to be done. I am elderly, and I am asking the police for some protection of my life and my property here. I am asking you for help."

The officer hastily took the information down and left. Several weeks later I called the police to find out what was happening with my complaint, and I was informed that they would not honor any restraining order of mine. I was taken aback.

After speaking with a member of the town council, whom I helped to get elected by working in her campaign, she advised me in confidence that Mr. Baldini was calling the shots, and that I should go to the mayor and complain. When I went to the mayor's office, I spoke with his secretary and was told, "The mayor is out of town, but you can speak to the mayor's assistant." I went into his office and told him my tale of woe, and he informed me, "You have been warned!"

I looked at him wide eyed and said, "Warned? Warned about what?"

"Yes," he said, "you need to get out of town. You are not welcome here."

I was born and raised in this town, I had lived here all of my life, I paid my taxes in a timely fashion, and he was warning me to get out of town. I got up from my chair, thanked him for his time and left his office. I went straight over to the mayor's secretary once again and asked, "When will the mayor be available?"

She advised what day he would be available, and I asked, "Please make an appointment for me. I want to speak with the mayor directly." The mayor was my husband's cousin.

On the appointed day, I arrived at the mayor's office a few minutes early. He invited me in, was cordial, and told me that he had invited Mr. Baldini and Detective Z, who was the head of the detective division at the police department. Mr. Baldini did not show up. Detective Z arrived but was late. I explained my situation and the reasons for the meeting. The mayor ordered a full investigation. And that seemed to be the end of that. The meeting was over. I was given no information on what to expect, no information on how long this would all take, and no information on how the outcome would be conveyed to me. The usual political tripe: order an investigation, and that would be where it would all end, because no one would ever know of the results. The usual safety net of politics ground in to motion. Things were no different.

One day in the middle of March, Melinda called me in the late afternoon and asked me to pick up Bryce at daycare, as she was running a little late. I picked him up, and we came home to find that Melinda had not arrived home yet. I decided to take a ride to the supermarket to recycle the plastic bags that had collected over the last several weeks. Bryce liked doing that chore with me. He liked poking those bags into the barrel. When we were finished, we got right back into the car and started to drive home. As we were driving down the street, we spotted Melinda's vehicle. She called me on the cell phone and asked me what we were doing. I told her what we did, and she said she would meet us at home.

Bryce and I drove straight home, and we waited and waited. Melinda never showed up. About an hour later, my doorbell rang, and when I opened the door, there stood a scruffy-looking man named David, who lived close to me, knew Melinda, and witnessed the events he was about to share with me.

When the police drove away with Melinda, he saw that they had abandoned her vehicle in an open condition, leaving behind her purse with a large sum of cash, her car keys, and other valuables. The man locked up her vehicle to protect its contents and took her keys that he was now handing to me. He told me, "Melinda has just been stopped by the police, pulled from her vehicle, searched, and thrown into the back of a police cruiser and taken away. I don't know anything more than this."

I stood there motionless. I never thanked him or spoke to him, and he left. I felt like somebody sucker punched me. I just stood there, numb and completely befuddled. I did not know what to do.

Bryce and I stood there and hugged each other. He was such a comfort, but I was sure he could feel my fear. The child began to speak to me and told me we needed to get mommy's car. His matter-of-fact behavior and the extent of his common sense for such a little boy shocked me back to reality.

I grabbed my purse and my grandson, and we walked the two blocks to where her vehicle had been left in order to drive it home. As we were walking down the street, a light drizzle was falling, and it was cold. I noticed Stefan had been flitting around outside his house, as if in anticipation of something. I was quite sure that he thought that his child would be with Melinda when she was arrested and that the police would take her into custody and bring the child to him or have him picked up at the station. His plans failed miserably.

Apparently, Stefan, having been unable to have Melinda incarcerated himself, now had his girlfriend, Olga, doing his dirty work for him. Olga filed a complaint with the police department that Melinda, on a particular day in March at nine o'clock in the evening, went over to Stefan's house and placed three cigars in the gas tank of her vehicle, which was parked facing the wrong way on the main thoroughfare in front of Stefan's house. She did not report that to the police as it was happening, but rather waited until the next day. She not only saw Melinda do this personally, but she told the police that a neighbor saw Melinda do it as well. We posted Melinda's bail to await arraignment in the district court, and we drove home. I begged Melinda not to take a plea agreement. This was just insane, and she should not have to plead to something that she did not do.

On the second day of April, Melinda appeared in court for arraignment. I was quite sure that I would not have to endure the wrath of the hanging judge by him ordering me to post excessive amounts of cash for bail. It was almost a certainty that Melinda would be incarcerated because she was on probation. That was terrifying in and of itself. On the day of arraignment, I conditioned myself mentally to see my daughter placed in those handcuffs once again and taken off to prison. I was strong for her, but I broke down once I left the courthouse. My worst fears had been realized. My stomach was in knots, and I could not move. I wanted to vomit. I was immobilized by the horror of what I had just experienced. I sat down on a bench outside the courthouse for some time before I could muster the strength to pick myself up and put one foot in front of the other and keep on walking to my vehicle.

The police were waiting for me when I arrived home. They barked, "Give us the child."

I asked, "Do you have a court order?"

They said, "We don't have one." They thought that I would just relinquish my precious grandchild to them because they were the police.

I was firm in my convictions—I said, "no order, no child!"

Later that afternoon, Stefan obtained a court order, and the police returned and took the child. We were not even allowed to say goodbye. He was just plucked from my arms and handed over, not to his father, but to the paternal grandmother. I imagined how awful this must have been for Bryce, constantly seeing his mother being dragged off by the police and constantly being plucked away from his loving family and being handed over to people who were not even nice to him—people he was afraid of.

My husband and I were just hollow shells and walked around like zombies. Stefan informed the daycare mother that Melinda took off and abandoned her child to go on an extended vacation. We never hid anything that had happened to us. We never hung our heads in shame. Our lives were an open book, and our neighbors and friends were supportive and sympathetic. The daycare mother told Stefan that she knew where Melinda was and how she got there. We were all in disbelief that a husband could do these awful things so many times to his wife. He called himself a man, but he was a whack job—nothing more.

Melinda's friend Ginger called me every day and told me what was going on with Melinda. Ginger worked in the criminal justice system prior to her marriage and was well connected there. She had been an absolute godsend for me. I had been so traumatized by all of this that I had not been able to work. My place of employment, which knew everything that had taken place, e-mailed me regularly, and they were gently pressuring me to return to work. It turned out to be a good persuasion. It had taken my mind off things and given me the opportunity to keep busy. On my first day back, everyone commented on how awful I looked.

Ginger gave me a telephone number that I needed to call to get directions to the prison and find out the procedures for visiting, telephoning, and incidentals. At five o'clock one morning, I called the telephone number that she had provided, thinking I was going to get a recording and that it would give me the information I needed. I was quite shocked to be speaking to a real-live correctional officer. I asked my questions through choked-back tears and was startled by his kindness.

The ride to the prison that afternoon was long and painful as I stoically contemplated what this experience would be all about and how it would all play out. I had never been to the prison before, and I followed the directions closely and with precision. As I get closer to the designated area, my eyes were filled with tears and my heart began to pound very fast as I attempted to understand my surroundings. I was encircled by buildings old and decrepit with high metal chain-link fences topped with coiled razor ribbon wire. Prisoners are out in the yard and well controlled—forbidden to look in my direction. I park my vehicle on the street in front of the prison, but I couldn't move from my vehicle. I was paralyzed by fear of what I saw. I wanted to get out of my car and rush right into the confines of that restricted area and see my child, but I was afraid of that next step now that I was there. I was held back by the unknown, and I was afraid. It took me a considerable amount of time to build up my courage before exiting my vehicle.

When I finally got in to the prison with Melinda's clothing for her court appearance, I was once again shaken as the guard threw them right back at me like they were garbage. "Unacceptable!" the guard barked.

They told me nothing and expected me to know all the rules and regulations. Being at a prison was a whole new experience for me, I thought. I looked at myself as someone better than that—these people here were different than me. But I was wrong and truly humbled when a tall black woman who was visiting her child took me under her wing and told me what the expectations were and gave me some coin change of her own to rent one of the lockers to place my jewelry in for safekeeping. She gently warned me to not wear anything of value when I visited. Wear old clothing and not more than necessary. It took me the entire first visit to comprehend what she was telling me. I was stripped of everything—jewelry, money, identification—everything. Her kindness and generosity overwhelmed me, and I was truly grateful. We were all truly kindred spirits joined by the circumstance of the moment, and there was genuine warmth in this very unusual bonding. Visiting hours were from six p.m. until eight p.m.

My biggest hurdle was getting through the metal detectors. No matter how much clothing the guards made me take off, I could not get past. Before long, I was standing there in a camisole bra and my underwear in front of the rest of the male and female visitors, whom I did not know, and still could not get past the detectors. I wondered to myself if it was really necessary to denigrate me in this manner, in front of people that I had never seen before. The guards were now convinced that I was attempting to sneak in contraband. I told them that there was nothing else I could possibly take off. I had nothing left, and I thought to myself that I would do whatever it took in order to have a visit with my child. I was a desperate woman. They would not win.

My thoughts continued as to what could possibly be next? Through my head ran the possibility of a strip search? I began to question myself as to whether or not I would submit. And as I was thinking this, it finally hit me. Many years ago I had corrective surgery on my left foot, and pins and screws held it together. They didn't believe that one either, but it was the best I could think to say in all honesty. However, they decided to scan my body. They moved that wand over my entire body at least thirty times, and the only time it beeped was when it came in close proximity with my left foot. By the time the guards finally made the decision to let me enter, it was well after seven p.m., and they called to end the visit at seven forty-five p.m. We both were crying during most of the visit, and our time together was short lived but oh, so precious.

I could not describe the conditions there in the prison because I was so nauseated by what I saw and what I heard and what I smelled, that I wanted to scream and run away as fast as I could. I had great difficulty holding back the tears. I was repulsed by the entire situation. Melinda had been in prison for about a week, and when I embraced her, her actions scared me. She rocked back and forth at the visiting table and cried uncontrollably. She was talking about suicide. Prior to her incarceration, Melinda took medications for her PTSD and severe depression. They had not allowed her any medication since she arrived. All medications were stopped cold turkey.

At the end of the visit, I spoke with the guard and inquired about the medication situation, and she told me in no uncertain words, "Tough break" and "don't plan on it." That said it all in a nutshell. I personally thought she could have been a little more diplomatic. Basically, she would not be allowed to take her medications. It was no wonder that people who were released from prison were so much worse off than when they went in.

I managed to get to my vehicle and roll down the windows. I sat there for some time, and I cried and cried and cried. I could not suck in enough cold air to relieve my abnormal breathing and fright. Composure was not a possibility for quite some time. I prayed to God to help us get through this. Melinda was strip-searched after every visit. And as hard as I tried to ignore the conditions of the prison, I did manage to discover what the rancid and rotting odor that I detected upon entering the visiting area that evening was. It was the bread that would be served to the inmates at the next day's meals. Morning coffee resembled "gray water" and was tasteless except for the subtle, fatty feel of it. Showers were communal, and the drains were often plugged with debris so that everyone stood in everyone else's effluent.

On the way home I stopped at Lily's house because Melinda had told me that Stefan visited with Lily and her boyfriend and had bragged about how he set Melinda up really good this time. The boyfriend was there and forbade Lily to speak with me. Even though I had never cared for this so-called friend, she always told me that she was a real friend to Melinda. I informed her that she was no friend, and I left. She called me very late that evening and left a message on my answering machine asking me to call her as she wanted to help. I called her, and we made arrangements to meet the next day. She did not show up for the meeting, and I never heard from her again. She would not help her friend by telling the truth, so how good of a friend was she?

It was impossible for me to sleep, and I went through the day trying to function but never really completing anything. I went from one thing to another to another, and I cried. Lily knew what the truth was, and she could save her friend, but her boyfriend forbade it. There is something wrong when people are afraid to speak because others are abusive and could hurt them. My heart was breaking, and there was not a thing that I could do. Our golden years were very much less than golden—all we saw was black. My hope was that someday we could look back on all of this and recognize it as a learning experience. We had always tried to see the good in people, and, since Melinda married Stefan, we realized that there were lots of bad, evil, vicious, and malicious people who surrounded us. My view of the world was very different than it had ever been.

Melinda's trial date finally arrived. Cousin Jesse, the psychologist, accompanied me to court so that she could be there emotionally for me. She and I sat on the left side of the gallery in the courtroom. We had no idea who Olga was, and we searched everyone sitting in the galleries. But after all of the cases had been heard and there were precious few people remaining in the gallery, we knew. It was the short woman with a dark complexion with the big, black, bulging eyes and the long, black, curly hair. She had a real look of evil about her.

The attorneys and the judge had a bench conference, and the judge kept insisting, "This matter needs to be dismissed." The assistant attorney general pressed on and insisted on a trial.

The judge stated, "It is a waste of the court's time, and I find it incredible that this woman could see clear around to the opposite side of her vehicle and see exactly what was being put in her gas tank at such a late hour from a window that was more than twenty feet from the vehicle. Yet she did not call the police. I find her actions to be impossible and there are no witnesses to support her claim. This case should be dismissed."

The attorney general doggedly persisted, "The state recommends Melinda be remanded back to prison for two more weeks to enable us time to find some witnesses."

The judge refused to allow that and once again told the prosecutor, "The state needs to dismiss its case."

The attorney general replied in the negative. Because the attorney general refused to dismiss for lack of proof and witness support, the judge announced, "Ready for trial!" Everyone hopped to attention. The judge banged his gavel and announced, "Case dismissed!"

Shortly after the judge's pronouncement, Olga got up out of her seat, jumped over the three or four people still seated in her row of the right gallery, and then lunged at Cousin Jesse and me yelling, "What did you say to me?" She yelled this phrase two or three times, then came at Cousin Jesse and me waving a clenched fist. Two sheriffs rushed her and escorted her out of the courtroom before any physical assault could take place. Cousin Jesse and I were shaking in our shoes. Melinda was now a free woman, and Cousin Jesse and I left the courthouse. As we were being escorted safely past Olga, she was heard on her cell phone calling the state police to file a complaint to have us arrested.

Later that afternoon, as Cousin Jesse and I sat around sipping on a glass of wine and reliving the day's events, the doorbell rang. It was a sheriff to serve me with papers. It was a restraining order filed by Olga. "A restraining order?" I did not even know that woman. I had never even seen her until this morning in the courtroom. Everything in that complaint was fabricated. Cousin Jesse and I realized that the sheriff was just doing her job, and she was so pleasant that we stood in the doorway of my home and talked to her for some time before bidding her good day.

Melinda had not seen her child in more than two weeks, and she stopped at the family court to regain custody of her son. Erin and Jim were not happy that the child was going back to his mother. They thought for certain that this was a done deal. Mom went to prison and the child was theirs. They were even more appalled when the child reached out to his grandfather and called for him. He jumped for joy when Pappa reached for him and scooped him up into his arms.

I immediately called Melinda on my cell phone so her little boy could say hello to his mommy. When we brought him into his house, he just kept looking around and was confused, like he was recognizing all of his stuff but thought he was never going to see it again. He slowly transitioned into the fun, loving child that he was prior to visiting with his father.

While I was on the Internet one night looking for an attorney to advise me as to how to protect ourselves from Stefan and his entourage and possibly filing a malicious prosecution lawsuit, I made the acquaintance of an attorney, and we just clicked. We communicated via e-mail for several weeks, and she told me that she was concerned for me going to court on the restraining order and not being represented by counsel. She would be there to represent me.

When we met in person, it was like meeting an old friend. She had the matter continued to the following week in order to give her more time to subpoena in the court report of the incident that happened in the courtroom during Melinda's trial where Olga was escorted out of the courtroom by the sheriffs when she tried to attack us. She wanted to subpoena in the sheriff herself, together with her report to be marked as evidence. Cousin Jesse and I went out to a nice restaurant after getting out of court. As we were talking and enjoying our meal, Melinda called me on my cell phone and told me about the big investigation going on in our neighborhood. The police had been out there taking pictures, measuring, and talking to people. They called my neighbor and asked her to give another statement about the incident that happened on March 7, when Stefan jumped the neighbor's fence and perched in her driveway with his camera and proceeded to stalk us. We were at the end of April, and they were just now getting around to an investigation? Something was going on, but I did not know if that was good or bad. I would just have to wait and see.

On Sunday, we had to pick up the baby at the police station, but we did not go straight home. We had some errands to run and did not arrive home until six forty-five p.m. When we pulled into our street, we noticed Olga's car parked out in front of Stefan's house and Jim's silver van was parked in Stefan's driveway. When we drove up the street toward the police station, there were no vehicles there. But when we pulled into our street, the whole of Stefan's family and guests were there. Knowing that Olga had a temporary restraining order against me, I could just imagine how they were conspiring against me to have me arrested for some trumped-up and manufactured allegations.

We went back to court for the hearing on the restraining order only to find out that it had once again been continued. One more day where I paid an attorney for doing nothing, it was becoming standard operating procedure. Cousin Jesse and I made the best of it and went out for lunch. Several days later we were back in court once again. It did not go well. The judge did not believe that I did not know this woman. I told the absolute truth, and the judge found my testimony to be heart wrenching but unbelievable. No one would file a restraining order against someone they did not know. He issued the restraining order in favor of Olga. It was clear for me to see that the courts did not want to hear the truth. The judges found the truth unbelievable. He then asked me if I had anything further to say, and I said yes, "I'm scared to death of this woman! I'm a senior citizen. I don't know this woman or anything about her. I'm afraid."

The judge also issued me a restraining order against Olga. The mutual restraining orders were for a period of ninety days.

About a week after the restraining orders were issued, I received a certified letter in the mail from Olga. I was so terrified as to what this could be that I had my attorney pick it up at the post office and sign for it. It was a motion Olga filed with the Superior Court to adjudge me in contempt of her restraining order, wherein she prayed for the courts to incarcerate me for a period of one year! I could not help but think that with my luck lately, I would not be surprised if they gave me life or even the death penalty. Why, that would seem only just for someone who had done nothing to that woman. I was hysterical and screaming at the top of my lungs. I could not take anymore. Who were these people?

On Mother's Day Melinda wished me a happy day and had her child wish me a happy day too. She dialed her mother-in-law's telephone number so the child could wish his other grandmother a happy day, and the mother-in-law hung up on her. Erin made such a nuisance out of herself in calling Melinda's employer that the state finally relented and filed a misdemeanor charge against Melinda.

The day after mother's day, we noticed that Stefan's vehicles were still at home and he had not gone to work and that Erin and Jim were at the house with him. We instinctively knew that something was up. When I arrived at work, I received a telephone call from Michael, telling me that the state police had arrested Melinda.

I called the state police, and they told me what was going on and that Melinda would be arraigned around eleven a.m. and would be released to await trial. But I knew only too well that Melinda was on probation, and that would not be the case. I left work and headed over to the courthouse so that I could be there for her. Melinda was once again incarcerated.

By the time the courts were finished dealing with her, it was midafternoon. I called Michael to come and pick me up. I never got over the pain of witnessing my child being placed in handcuffs and dragged off in plain view, as if she were something less than human. It was always with me, no matter how many times I had experienced it. That nerve was forever raw and would remain unhealed. Once again, I felt like my guts had been ripped out of me, and, once again Melinda, in an even more fragile state than the previous incarceration, was taken off her medications while she awaited trial.

Michael had been watching our grandchild since Melinda had been taken away in handcuffs earlier in the morning, in front of her child. We were both in a daze. From the moment we arrived back, Stefan started stalking us in his vehicle and was yelling at us. He pursued us wherever we went. At 3:04 p.m., I called the police department and reported Stefan was stalking us, and I had a restraining order. The way the police officer responded to me, I distinctly got the impression that they knew there was something going on. They told me to come directly to the police station. Because I was afraid of Stefan and the police, I called them back at 3:06 p.m. and asked them to dispatch a police officer to my home. Michael went into the house with Bryce.

Officer Pisschitzski was dispatched to my home and pulled up in front. Stefan was now in his jeep and on the corner, in front of my neighbor's house. I went out my front door and up to the police cruiser to talk to the officer. As I approached the police vehicle, I realized that Stefan's vehicle was a lot closer to me than it had been, and then as I was leaning into the window of the police vehicle I became aware that Stefan's vehicle was moving. I attempted to protect myself, and, as I turned to run, the driver's side corner of his bumper struck me on the right knee, and I was splayed onto the hood of Stefan's vehicle. As I got myself off the vehicle, I said to the officer, "He just hit me with his vehicle."

Officer Pisschitzski said to me "Oh no, I saw you jump!"

I was thinking to myself, *I'm a senior citizen standing between two vehicles that are approximately eighteen inches apart. I would have had to jump straight up in the air to have jumped onto his hood. At my age, that would be considered truly a miracle.*

At that time I did not know that I had been injured and proceeded to speak with the officer. There was no question that we were being hunted and stalked by Stefan, but the police were not inclined to hear anything about it. The police were so pre-occupied being involved in a civil matter that they were not of a mindset to deal with a crime. It was only after Officer Piss-chitzski told me to call Sergeant Sullivan, and I was hobbling up to my front door to do so, that I realize that my knee had been split open from the impact and that I was bleeding. Michael, horrified by what he was witnessing, watched the entire incident from the front porch.

I came into my house, and I called Sergeant Sullivan from my home phone. At three seventeen p.m. Sergeant Sullivan, in a voice fierce and demanding, ordered, "You must relinquish control over your grandson to Stefan."

I asked him, "Do you have a court order?"

He said, "Yes, there is a court order!"

When I asked him for a copy of it, he could not produce it. He tried to intimidate me and said, "I will write a report that you are uncooperative."

I said, "You should try telling the truth and upholding the law. This is your job."

At three twenty-six p.m. I called Melinda's attorney, and he said, "Do not relinquish the child without a court order."

I went back outside to Office Pisschitzski and told him, "No court order? No child."

At three forty p.m. I called Melinda's attorney and once again explained the situation, and he again said, "Do not relinquish the child." Pisschitzski called for backup, and he and Officer New-ton stood on the corner of my street and the main thorough-fare laughing and joking around with Stefan for a considerable amount of time and eventually left.

At five twenty p.m. another officer showed up at my door with his partner officer. Michael and I went outside with the child. They told me they now had a court order that had just been issued by the court shortly after five p.m. for the child. They were very polite.

I asked, "May I take that order into the house and make a copy of it and change the baby and bring him out with the original order?"

He told me, "Take your time. We can wait." I made the copy, changed the baby, and made my way outside to hand the child to the police officer.

In Officer Pisschitzski's statement and report, he stated that Michael was outside yelling racial slurs at him and screaming at him. However, in a subsequent report, he stated that there was no one else present and that there were no witnesses to the incident.

I visited with my child every visitation day, and she called me several times daily from the prison. She did nothing but cry, and she was very scared. Sometimes I cried with her, and sometimes I was very scared. But mostly all I could do was be there to listen to her and be her beacon in the darkness. Our family unit was strained beyond belief. How we would survive, I did not know. The only thing I knew for sure was that we were a strong, committed family, and by the grace of God, we would survive that.

Cousin Jesse and I arrived at the courthouse with the attorney so that I could answer the contempt complaint of Olga. In her complaint, she stated that I had violated the restraining order by calling her place of business and repeatedly harassing her. I had caused her considerable financial hardship. Her mother had a stroke, her brother had to have open-heart surgery and was in serious condition. She was infertile, and that all of that was brought on by me. And, of course, she thought that I should be incarcerated for a minimum of one year. I looked at that, and I was convinced that that was some sort of joke. How could I possibly be responsible for all of these things she had accused me? I did not even know that woman.

Olga was now represented by an attorney, and the judge was seriously considering the one-year incarceration. I could not fathom how a judge could be so taken in by these bogus allegations as to be seriously considering incarceration.

The two attorneys met in chambers with the judge. After several hours of closed-door hearings, my attorney told me that I needed to bring in all of my home telephone and cell phone records to prove that I did not do anything. Olga was the plaintiff, and the burden of proof was upon her to prove that I had done something. However, the judge made it incumbent upon me, the defendant, to prove that I did not do anything wrong. I thought to myself that something was askew here, some sort of double standard. I felt violated. I explored the possibility of going to prison for something I did not do and because of a person I did not know. How could that be possible?

One week later, we were back in court again, and I had volumes of papers containing all my cell phone records, my husband's cell phone records, my home telephone records, and my business telephone records, both incoming and outgoing calls, for the last year. It took the attorneys an entire day to scrutinize and evaluate every line of every bill. However, when all was said and done, there was not one telephone call made by me to Olga either at her business or at her home. The attorneys once again met with the judge in chambers. My attorney told the judge that Olga was the girlfriend of a person who was related to me, and we were involved in a custody issue in the family court. She apprised him of the things she had done in order to gain a favorable verdict for her boyfriend in the family court by lying and making things up.

When the judge took the bench to make a ruling on the contempt motion, he made note and addressed the court as follows: "There is no way for the plaintiff to prove any of her allegations. He is hard-pressed to see how the defendant could have caused your mother's stroke, and there would be no way to substantiate that the defendant was the cause of your infertility."

He could clearly see from the records presented that there was not one violation of contact, and she could not produce any evidence of financial loss. He further stated, "I find your complaint to be not provable." He did, however, look at me square in the eye and declared, "The restraining order will remain in full force and effect until the next hearing date. You must obey. I would not even think twice about throwing you in prison!"

I sat there with tears running down my face, as I softly said, "Thank you, Your Honor."

On Tuesday, the thirteenth of May, I received a telephone call from Detective Z. He asked me if he could come to my home around ten thirty a.m. to discuss the findings of his investigation. He informed, "I will be issuing a 'no trespass' order to Stefan so that he can't go into your neighbor's yard to annoy you anymore, and the attorney general's office had declined the violation of restraining order."

I asked, "How does issuing a no trespass order to my neighbor protect me from my rights being violated?"

He said, "I presented the findings of my investigation to the attorney general, and that's the best that the attorney general could come up with!"

I deemed it fair. I said to Detective Z, "If you presented your findings to the attorney general, then you were misguided by presenting only one side of the story."

At no time did anyone come to me or speak to me during the investigation, and at no time was I allowed to tell my side of the story, although I saw you all out there during that investigation and made myself available to be interviewed at any point during that investigation. But that did not happen.

I filed the complaint against Stefan; I had the restraining order. I was the one being harassed, and I was the one being stalked by him. Detective Z said, "I did not know that you were involved in that incident. The police report written by the responding officer indicated that my neighbor called the police and that she complained."

I said, "This is a complete fabrication on the responding officer's part."

He took some further notes, and he could see that I was in serious pain from the injury sustained when Stefan hit me with his vehicle. He suggested, "You should see a doctor." And then he left.

Later that afternoon Detective Z called me and asked me if I could come into the station the next day and file a formal complaint and allow him to take pictures of my knee injury and some measurements. I was happy to oblige and was filled with new hope.

I went to visit with my child that evening and was told by the entry guards there would be no visit. Melinda had been moved to the I Building. I internalized that the "I" must mean isolation of some sort. They would give me no information, and fear devoured me. I was afraid that she might have tried to hurt herself because her self-esteem was so low and she could not take any more, either physically or mentally. Michael tried to comfort me on the ride home. He instinctively knew what that was doing to me inside. When I arrived home, I began to frantically call the prison for any and all news of my daughter. But they were not forthcoming. I began to scream at the top of my lungs, "I want my life back. I want my family to be whole again! Please, dear God, help us! God have mercy on us and forgive us for whatever it was that we may have done—ever in our lives. Forgive us!"

I went to the police station the next day, as I promised to file a complaint with Detective Z. He was very thorough in his investigation. He proceeded to share with me a personal situation that he had in his own family, and I really thought that we connected. He made up a complaint against Stefan, and he took pictures of the injury to my knee and made measurements as to the location on my leg of the injury and its correlation to the bumper height of Stefan's vehicle. I spent the entire morning with him, and I shook his hand as I readied to leave. I thought him to be sincere, as he told me, "I would like for something to come of this and see Stefan get his just desserts."

He asked, "How is Melinda doing in prison?" I could not answer him, as I was overcome with emotion. He sensed my grief and squeezed my hand and told me, "Everything is going to be okay. He is going to present this to his boss, and we'll be in touch soon."

Cousin Jesse came over really early Friday, May the twenty-eighth. It was the day that Melinda would be tried on the state's misdemeanor charge of filing a false report. I had not been allowed to visit with my child, and I wanted to get to the courthouse early. The courtroom was pretty full, even though we were early. All of Stefan's family was there to witness Melinda being brought into the courtroom in shackles and handcuffs, and many from protective services were there.

It was not long before the prisoners were pulled in, handcuffed and shackled, like garbage headed to the dump. I spotted Melinda. She was thin, her face unrecognizable, red, and her eyes were swollen and puffed shut from uncontrollable crying. Her body was shaking, and tears poured down her cheeks. The posture of her body told me that she had given up—there was no fight left in her. I put my hand to my mouth to silence my gasp of horror, and the sheriff put Jesse and I out of the courtroom for my display of shock at seeing my child. My heart sank. *I must be there—this is my child.*

We had been trying to watch through a small window in the door to the courtroom and after a few minutes of being excluded, Cousin Jesse and I nonchalantly walked back into the courtroom and sat down ever so quietly, so as not to draw attention to ourselves. When the sheriff finally spotted us again, he came and escorted us out once more. I was hysterical. As we were peering in through the window, we saw the female sheriff go over to the male sheriff who banned us and whispered something in his ear. He instantly turned and motioned us back into the courtroom with a black, leather-gloved hand. We were allowed back in just in time to hear Melinda plead guilty to a crime she had not committed. She received a one-year suspended sentence and one year of probation, but she would be incarcerated for ninety days for violation of probation.

The very next day, after a day of hard work, I was determined to see my child at the prison. Michael drove me there, as he wanted to feel close to her. We arrived early, and we just sat quietly, looking at each other but not saying a word. If I had tried to speak, I knew I just would have cried, and I did not want to do that. I wanted to look positive and upbeat for my daughter so that I could encourage her. When it was time for the visit, they would not allow me in because I was wearing sandals. Determined to have a visit with my child come hell or high water, I ran back out to the truck and grabbed the shoes off Michael's feet and ran back to the prison, bare footed, his size 14EEEE shoes in hand. I put them on my feet when I reached the checkpoint. All of the visitors were laughing, and I explained, "You have to do what you have to do!" Nothing would prevent me from seeing my child.

Our lives consisted of taking care of Melinda's apartment, taking care of her animals, paying her bills, and taking care of everything else for her. We talked to her several times daily via telephone, but this was not a life. I worked, took care of my personal business and home, and worked hard trying to live a normal life. We had not been allowed to see our grandchild and had resigned ourselves to the fact that we might never be allowed to see him again. Stefan had been awarded sole custody of the child at long last. All we had left of him were stolen moments that the daycare mother allowed us. She had been so kind to us. We would go without notice, and she always allowed us a few minutes where he jumped into Pappa's arms, and he hugged us. He rested his little head on my chest and begged, "Where's Mommy?"

We soothed him, and we said, "Mommy loves you very, very much, but she can't be with you right now."

We put on our happy faces so Bryce would not know that anything was wrong. And, when it was time to leave him, we always promised to try to see him again. It was a promise that we were unsure that we would be able to keep, but it was all that we could offer that innocent child. A two-year-old child should not have to worry about his family. We sat in our vehicle, and we both cried. We did not understand how one man and his entourage could do this to another human being or to an entire family, and—worst of all—to his own child.

Melinda had now been moved to minimum security, and her divorce attorney had petitioned the court for a visit with her child. During each successive stolen visit with our grandchild, we became more and more aware that his speech had regressed, and we were unable to understand what he was saying. His growth had been stunted, and he seldom laughed. We were very worried about him. There was something very wrong. I was working diligently to get visits for Bryce with his mommy. Every week it was a new excuse. Stefan did not have the child. His mother and stepfather had the child, and he only visited with him occasionally, but he was calling the shots because he had sole custody.

Finally, word came that we could pick up the little boy at daycare on Thursday, July 3, and we could have him visit with us for the weekend. This was such a momentous happening for us. We were so exhilarated. We would be able to take him for his first visit with his mommy on Thursday evening, and then we could head off to our boat and be with the little one to watch the fireworks on the Fourth and then have another visit with Mommy on Sunday evening before we had to return him to his father.

We spent the next several days packing our truck for our cherished adventure. Cloud nine would have adequately described our happiness. As we continued readying for the upcoming weekend, at six thirty on Wednesday evening, Melinda's attorney called us and told us Stefan had reneged, and we would not be allowed a visit. As we went outside to lock the garage, there was Stefan standing at the fence with his child held high in the air and was thrusting him in and out like a shield of some victorious soldier

Louise Baron-Kent

and yelling over to Michael, "You are a coward, a liar, and you have no balls." When Stefan vehemently began berating Melinda and I, Michael took off his fanny pack, laid it on his truck, and walked over to Stefan's yard. Stefan immediately got on the phone and called 911 and told the police, "Michael is assaulting me both physically and verbally as we speak."

Michael never said a word to him, nor did he touch him. He knelt down with the child and began to cry. He whispered into the child's ear, "I tried, and I failed, and I am sorry." Many neighbors were outside and saw what had happened. Stefan was trying to get each and every neighbor to say that Michael struck him.

It was not long before the police arrived and placed Michael under arrest. Many of the neighbors told the police that there was no assault. They refused to take any statements, and they refused to speak with Michael to see what had happened. As they were driving away with Michael in the backseat, the police yelled at the neighbors, "If you have something to say, tell it to the mayor!" We should have known that this would be the retaliatory event that we had to suffer for having gone to the mayor to fight for our rights and complain about the police.

Michael posted his bail and was released. The next day was spent on the telephone, talking to neighbors and friends who called in disbelief of such a thing happening, because, of course, this was big news to the police, and it was plastered all over the newspapers: a man who had led an exemplary life for sixty-three years and was a real true life "gentle giant" was arrested for assault.

We went to the daycare that afternoon and had one of our stolen moments with our grandchild. He jumped into Pappa's arms. His body was shaking he got so excited. He kept saying to us, "Mema, I want to live with you! Please take me with you!"

We hugged and reassured him, "We love you very much, but we are not allowed to take you with us."

When our time was up, he said, "Mema, wait," and he walked over to a pile of toys and produced a small etch-a-sketch. On it he drew a smiley face, and we melted. As he left us at the door, his mood became very sullen and withdrawn. It was sheer torture for us, as adults, to deal with all that was happening to us. I could just imagine what it must be like for such a small child who probably thought the people that he loved most had abandoned him.

It was during a visit with my elderly neighbor to check on her that I realized that I had heard nothing from the police department and made a mental note to follow up. My neighbor was very afraid of Stefan, and I wanted to make sure that she was doing all right. Stefan had a way of bullying the elderly and making them very afraid. She was a frail woman, and I worried about her. She hugged me and with tears in her eyes, said, "I am more afraid for Michael and you than I am for myself." She sympathized with our situation and vowed to help in any way she could.

All was not lost for this weekend, however. An emergency order issued by the court ordered Stefan to make the child available at the police station at four thirty p.m. on Sunday and to be returned to the police station at eight thirty p.m. Jim dropped him off at the appointed time and admonished, "Michael is not to be around this child." I forced a smile in compliance.

Who did he think he was? He and his wife, Erin, refused to let me drive off alone. They were staying right behind my vehicle and had intended to supervise our visit and to make sure that Michael was not a part of it. I refused to move my vehicle, and I called the police station. When they saw the police officer coming out, they then took off in a huff. I drove around for a few minutes to make certain that I was not being followed.

I picked up Michael at our home, and we drove to the prison and had a wonderful visit with Melinda and her child. It saddened Melinda to see how much her child had regressed. He talked only baby talk now and had reverted back to wearing diapers at the age of two and a half. The child was so happy to see his mother. He would not let her put him down. He stayed firmly planted on her lap, and he hugged her, kissed her, and for the moment, life was good for him.

I followed up on my mental note that I made to myself regarding the police station, as I had not heard from Detective Z. My hope was all but gone. I called him on several occasions, and he did not have the common courtesy of returning my phone calls. I sent him an e-mail asking him the outcome of the investigation and only half expected any response from him. He eventually sent me an e-mail and told me he was forbidden to open a case under my restraining order complaint. To me it was perfectly clear—Baldini! So this was how the investigation and disposition of my complaint ended, just as I thought.

There subsequently had been several other instances where Stefan's behavior was so offensive and frightening that I sought out help from the police. At one point, I printed out a copy of the stalking statutes for our state and filed them with my complaint. The police did nothing to help us but did have an officer call me to explain that my restraining order would never be honored, and that I should know that from my previous attempts to get it enforced. Their conditioning of us was complete. I never called the police again for anything. My resolve was to hold my head high and to remain a resident. Stefan, Baldini, or the police would not intimidate me.

During a successive visit, Bryce announced, "Mema, I want to go home—to our home." We complied with his request. We thought that perhaps he wanted to play outside in his own yard, with his own things, but he did not. He wanted to come inside, and he was very insistent. He sat down at his table and chairs in the foyer, and he looked around, and the memories of his life here came flooding back to him.

He asked me, "Can I hold that?" as he pointed to the glass globe that changes colors. As he went to pick it up off the pie safe, where it rested, the pie safe tipped and the globe fell to the floor. He was out of control with hysteria and was sure something awful would befall him.

I pulled him close to me and reassured him, "It's all right—it was an accident."

He would not be consoled, he just cried and hugged me and said, "I'm sorry, Mema."

I laid him across my chest and kept telling him, "I love you, Bryce," and rubbed his back to soothe him. I truly thought it was a release of some sort for him, and he realized that Mema and Pappa were still in his life, and we had not gone away.

As we hugged, he spotted the gel flags that he had stuck on the glass of my front exit door. We had not done anything to that front window since he put those there. Every fingerprint, every handprint, every smudge were just as he had left them. They were our special memories that we had of him, and just in case we never were allowed to see him again, it sustained us. We sometimes just sat and looked at his wonderful artwork and remembered his vibrancy and being. It had been several months since we had seen him, and it broke our hearts. The thought of him being removed from our lives forever by his father saddened us greatly. It was more than we could bear. It took away our reason for living.

During the time of Melinda's incarceration, Stefan and his family pressured the family court judge to have a hearing on the divorce, knowing full well that Melinda would be brought into court in handcuffs and shackles. I'm sure just the thought of them further humiliating Melinda like that left them intoxicated with heightened gratification and titillating in pure pleasure. The judge acquiesced to their requests and scheduled the hearings on several occasions during this period of time, and I could just imagine their glee.

However, it was the month of July, and I believed he inwardly realized that nothing much happened at the courthouse during the summer months unless it was an absolute emergency. Every time a scheduled date neared, it was continued to another date several weeks down the line.

The hearing date for the disposition of Olga's restraining order against me was a day that I had been awaiting with trepidation on one side but great hope on the other. It was the day that was pre-scheduled for the review and possible vacating of the restraining order that Olga obtained against me three months ago. Olga never showed up for court and neither did her attorney. Neither did they have the common courtesy to call the court to either reschedule or offer a reason for not being in attendance. The clerk was of the mind that she would reschedule it, which would further my anxieties by prolonging the torture. She went to discuss the matter with the judge and came out in short order and announced, "The judge will take the bench!"

I was thinking that with my luck, the way it had been for the last several years, he would come out to the bench and announce that, out of fairness, he would notify the plaintiff and plaintiff's attorney that they failed to show up for the hearing and that it was now rescheduled to a time that was more convenient for them. To my amazement, he ascended the bench in his usual stoic manner and began his dissertation. He commenced, "In all my years on the bench, I pride myself on always being on time. I abhor people who think it absolutely fine to keep others waiting and uninformed as to a reason for their tardiness. My calendar reflects that this particular date was pre-selected three months prior for review and possible termination barring any violation of the restraining order. I make note here for the record that Olga filed a motion to adjudge you in contempt but that her claim was ridiculous, and there is no possible way for her to substantiate it. Madame Attorney, what is your pleasure here?"

My attorney reiterated all of the facts that the judge had noted and asked, "I ask for the court to issue an order to vacate the restraining order."

The judge applauded her for being correct in her assessment and issued an order vacating the original restraining order. Off the record, before exiting the bench, the judge looked at me and stated, "I detest people who use the various courts for their own personal pleasure or purpose. I acknowledge that I now know that you had been telling the truth from the beginning." He attempted to justify his position and the difficulties of deciding who was truthful and who was not. He wished me luck as I stood there with tears running down my face. My attorney and I both thanked him for his wisdom, and we left.

Stefan had discontinued the visits for the child to visit with his mother. Melinda had not seen her child for more than fifty-six days. His reasoning for not allowing the visits to continue was because we had arrived home fifteen minutes early one Sunday and did not return the child to him forthwith. How would

Louise Baron-Kent

he know that? But the good news was she would be released from prison on the last day of July, well in time for the next family court hearing on the first day of August. She would not be there in handcuffs and shackles as Stefan and his family had so hoped. She would be there a free woman.

We had our second pre-trial conference with the prosecutor for Michael's assault charge on the morning that Melinda was being released. The prosecutor, during the first pre-trial in which he spoke with our witnesses, alluded to the fact that he did not want to prosecute. However, he scheduled a second hearing so that he could speak with the victim, Stefan. When he finished talking to his witness and he subsequently appointed a victim advocate to Stefan, no words were necessary. Stefan had insisted on prosecution to the full extent of the law. We would be back at some later date for a full trial.

The Road to Freedom

2008

August 1, 2008, we arose early and got ready for the family court hearing. We arrived early and took our place in the courtroom. The judge took the bench and cleared the courtroom. Stefan's family sat outside in the hallway, and I took a place in the ante-room so that I could see what was going on and not have to be near that family. Olga was called as the first witness and, of course, as expected, she lied about everything. She even went as far as to testify, "Melinda's mother is such an awful person and has done such awful things to me that I found it necessary to get a restraining order against her."

Melinda's attorney informed her, "There is no restraining order."

She became quite argumentative and insisted, "There most certainly is one!" She was so cocky. It was then that she learned, much to her surprise, that the order had been vacated. She went on to testify, "Stefan is a wonderful person and a wonderful father." She further stated, "I never slept over when the child was present, and when we were on vacation, I stayed in a separate hotel."

When Stefan testified it was more of the same as his girlfriend, one lie after another. We were in the courthouse all day, and it was a grueling experience for us. Our next family court hearing was scheduled for Tuesday, as the judge was in the habit of taking Mondays as vacation days.

The judge ordered a weekend visitation for Melinda, commencing at eight a.m. on Saturday until Melinda asked for six p.m. on Sunday. But the judge ordered seven thirty p.m. on Sunday. That was a gift. We thought it the perfect opportunity for all of us to get away and spend the weekend on our boat.

We all had such a wonderful and relaxing weekend. It was a welcome opportunity for us all to reconnect after Melinda's release from prison. The little boy just loved sleeping on the boat, and he loved driving the dinghy. At least once an hour, we had to take a harbor cruise, so he and his Pappa took to the helm. He brought no toys with him, and he was not bored for one second. There was so much for him to explore on this boat that he ran out of time before it was time for him to leave.

On Sunday morning little Bryce was standing at our stateroom door yelling, "Get up, Pappa!"

Pappa and Bryce had breakfast together and left for a private harbor cruise of their own. This little boy squealed with joy from the moment of arrival until the time of his departure. When it was time for him to go back to his father, he screamed and screamed, "No, Mommy! No, Mommy! I want to stay with you, Mommy!"

This just ripped our hearts out. What kind of people took a small child away from such a good mother? They lied and lied and needed to win at all costs. Bryce was nothing more than the prize. They didn't care about him—he was just the trophy.

On Tuesday I decided that I would work in the city so that I would be close at hand in case that should be the day that I would testify. I ended up working all day but never got the call to come and have my say. Melinda and I did, however, manage a pleasant and relaxing lunch at one of our favorite restaurants, and we traveled home together.

On Wednesday, it was the same scenario. Work in the city and be prepared to give testimony. At eleven a.m. I was called to the courthouse to testify. When I arrived, the judge announced that he would resume after lunch, as he wanted to hear a quick case in between.

Melinda and I welcomed the opportunity to have lunch together once again and headed over to "10," a really good restaurant near the courthouse. We were not getting much accomplished in court, but we were sure eating well.

When we arrived back at the courthouse at two p.m., and I was called to testify, the judge said, "I am bored with this case and do not want to hear any more of this trial." He suggested, rather strongly, "All of the parties and their respective attorneys go out into the hall and try to work things out on your own, and I am ordering a schedule of visitation be worked out by the parties and work through my appointee, as I am leaving for the day."

Later that afternoon, we found out that Olga had filed a complaint against Melinda citing death threats and a physical attack in the courthouse. Both her attorney and I had been with her all day, and we left the courthouse together, and no such thing had happened. I instinctively knew that something bad was about to happen. That evening I slept in little Bryce's bedroom. I wanted to be warmed by his presence. I needed to do this just in case I never got to feel him again. With Stefan anything was possible. My faith had been shaken to its core, and if that did become reality, then I would know that there was *no God!*

The very next day, Melinda called me at work and told me she was going over to the superior courthouse at two p.m. and filing a restraining order against Olga, and she asked me if I would come with her. When we arrived at the courthouse, Olga was there, filing a restraining order against Melinda. It was a mutual restraining order that issued and was completed in short order. We had no way of knowing that, once again, Olga had gone to the capital police and filed a complaint of disorderly conduct against Melinda.

It was not long after that when the police began surveillance on our home and calling Melinda on her cell phone. I immediately called Melinda's attorney who, in turn, called the police, only to find out that there were two warrants for her arrest. What we later learned through the attorney was that the police could not issue the warrant because the two incidents happened in another city, and the judge refused to violate Melinda. But Olga went to an attorney who presented the case to another judge who overrode the first judge and obtained a bench warrant for a "felony stalking."

Olga's attorney called Melinda's probation officer at least a dozen times trying to get Melinda violated. Melinda's attorney was determined to track down the attorney general and get this matter straightened out. As the criminal attorney was exchanging information with the divorce attorney, it became crystal clear. The divorce attorney suddenly remembered the incident. He remembered that it was Olga who lunged at Melinda and was restrained by Jim. Melinda did not do or say anything to Olga, and he would be more than happy to testify, as an officer of the court, to that fact.

Melinda's attorney and I worked out a plan that would keep Stefan and Olga out of the loop of knowing that Melinda was being arrested and possibly re-incarcerated. Had Stefan known for sure that was the day, he would have informed the police so that he could be there to watch and jubilate as he usually did. He watched our house constantly, and he knew every move we made.

We designated a particular destination for meeting once we were able to get out of our neighborhood while under Stefan's watchful eye. Our travel that morning would be very convoluted. Michael walked out of our house and to the corner of our street, and, low and behold, Stefan came running out of his house and tried to engage Michael.

Michael turned and headed back to our house. I walked out of our house with briefcase in hand and got into my vehicle, and Stefan was out of his house and in his vehicle faster than I could start mine. He attempted to follow me, but I made two successive and unexpected turns, and he suddenly was no longer there. I kept on going and making more turns. And finally, I parked my automobile in a cluster of vehicles in a church parking lot.

I called Michael, who was now walking our neighborhood on foot, and he reported that Stefan had been driving up and down the main thoroughfare and checking the side streets, but he was nowhere in sight. Believing we finally evaded him, I approached our house from a different direction and pulled into my rear driveway, where Melinda was waiting, and we headed out in a different direction from where I believed Stefan might have gone.

We arrived at our predetermined destination without notice of either the police or Stefan. We were at the courthouse all day and were informed that the attorney general added a third charge for some event unbeknownst to us. After everything was said and done, and being unable to work things out with the attorney general, and after much crying, screaming, and praying, Melinda was forced to turn herself in, once again, for something she had not done and would, once again, be incarcerated.

Her attorney recognized the fact that she was suicidal. We were sure that she would not survive that ordeal, and that is the very worst nightmare for any parent. Prior to turning herself in, she asked me to prepare her last will and testament and any and all papers necessary for expedient disposition of any and all of her worldly possessions, and they were properly executed at the courthouse before she was led away in handcuffs. She knew that I would take care of her son regardless of who had custody of him. He was a child and had no say, but one day he would be able to speak for himself. We all kept on fighting, but each and every time we were down, they just kept on kicking us. Where would it all end? My stress and anxiety levels were so high that I believed that one day I would just drop dead.

Melinda's attorney and I spent the remainder of that afternoon doing legwork. We went to the superior courthouse to find out any information that we could about Olga's complaint there.

When she came out, she told me she had good news and she had bad news. I said, "Just tell me straight out, I have no energy for guessing games." The good news was that everything Olga complained to the capital police about never happened, and the bad news was that Olga was there at the courthouse filing a motion to adjudge Melinda in contempt of their restraining order. She then advised me, "We're going to the district court and filing a restraining order against Stefan." We picked up the paperwork for the restraining order, went to a restaurant and filled them out, and after lunch went to the courthouse and filed them. To my amazement, the judge signed them immediately, and we were on our way. This was quite shocking compared to the first time I went there without an attorney.

On our way home that evening, we noticed in our rearview mirror that Stefan was following us. Everywhere we went, he was right behind us. I spoke with Melinda's attorney about this, and she advised we go to the police station and file stalking charges. But what would be the point? They would do nothing. We did go to the police as advised and filed a report for felony stalking, and, just as suspected, the police did nothing.

At the end of August, Melinda had her trial for the three complaints filed against her by Stefan's stepfather and Stefan's girlfriend, Olga. There was absolutely no truth to what they complained of, so I thought we were going to sit back and watch these two people perjure themselves. The vicious lies that came out of their mouths made my blood boil. Olga testified to the fact that Melinda came right up to her and punched her in the chest and said she was "as good as dead."

I was with Melinda, and I did not see her do this. Her attorney testified that this did not happen, and when Jim got up to testify, he gave a completely different account than Olga. The judge who presided at the trial was dealing with an ongoing situation very similar to ours within his own family, and perhaps was not the best of judges to hear that case. He did, however, dismiss two of Olga's complaints because there was not a shred of evidence to support any of them. However, he went on to say that people just do not file complaints for no reason. He found their lies to be credible, and even though there was no evidence whatsoever, he said that Melinda "must be guilty of something" and found her guilty of disorderly conduct.

It was a sad day in the judiciary when an officer of the court was not believed but two psychopaths were found to be credible. I was in complete shock. I could not believe what I was hearing. He gave her a one-year suspended sentence and one year of probation with ninety days to serve for being a probation violator. Melinda's attorney immediately filed an appeal to the superior court. Melinda was taken away in handcuffs once again and sent back to prison. My husband and I were so dumbfounded that we were paralyzed by the horror we had just witnessed.

Our body language said it all. We could barely walk upright to get out of the courthouse. We were inconsolable and did not want to speak to or look at anyone. Fear and apprehension consumed our beings. We did not even look at each other. We were beyond supporting each other emotionally. How was it possible to keep on going? When would enough be enough? There were no words to adequately describe the thoughts that were going through our minds. My heart went out to my child. She was in an even further despondency than either of us. The depths of her despair were unfathomable to us.

Two days later, Labor Day weekend, Melinda's attorney called me to ask for a favor. I said certainly, "I can help, what is it that you need me to do?"

She said, "I need to know the width of the main thoroughfare and the width of each sidewalk of this thoroughfare in our area of town for an accident reconstruction scene."

Since she lived in the southern end of the state and I lived right here, it would save her a considerable amount of time in driving up to measure for herself. We were on our way to the boat, it was a holiday weekend, and there was no traffic, so I decided to do it immediately.

Running into the house, I got my tape measure and went out to the main road with Michael and completed this task in short order, no more than five minutes. A former friend and Mother Superior of a religious community was driving through my neighborhood and saw me and stopped to say hello, as I had not seen her in several years.

She was stopped at the corner of my street, and we were talking when the police showed up. It was Stefan's friend, Officer Pisschitzski. He drove right up to Michael, who still had my camera dangling from his wrist from loading the truck for our holiday weekend, and demanded, "Give me the camera."

My friend and I were standing just several feet away. I apologized to her and excused myself and went into my yard and took the camera from Michael. Officer Pisschitzski yelled, "Give that camera to me!"

I looked him in the eye and asked, "Who do you think you are?" I said, "This is my camera, and I will be taking it into my house, and I will be calling my attorney and telling her about your bullying, and then I will be calling the police station and reporting you."

I went into the house to put the camera in safekeeping, and as I was walking back out, Officer Pisschitzski spoke into the mike perched on his shoulder and a voice spit back at him. "Leave him alone!"

Officer Pissschitzski rudely said to Michael, "This is your lucky day." He got into his police cruiser and began to pull away, and, as he did, he shouted, "I will be reporting you to the state police." We just looked at him and shook our heads that this officer could act in such an unprofessional manner.

My friend could not believe the way the police treated us. I made her aware of what was going on, and I said that behavior was nothing. That was pretty mild compared to how they usually treated us. My friend, Michael, and I spent that weekend on our boat rekindling our relationship and divulging events of the past several years to her.

On Sunday evening, when we went to visit with Melinda at the prison, Michael was not allowed in. Because the incarceration was considered a new episode, they did a new criminal background check on both of us. The arrest record of Michael for the alleged assault showed up, and he no longer would be able to visit with his daughter. Melinda and I had a great visit and laughed a little and joked around a little and talked about serious issues also. There was no crying, and it felt good for a change. She told me, "I am determined to keep on fighting no matter how long it takes. I am resigned to the fact that things may not go in my favor because they are all such good liars, but I am going to keep on fighting."

"I will be right by your side," I said.

Some of my neighbors called me later in the evening to tell us that the police had been watching our house all weekend. One neighbor told me that they drove by at least once an hour. I guess they were making sure we were being controlled adequately or that Stefan was not being inconvenienced. We did not care any longer. This was pure harassment on their part, but we did not care.

While telling my story to my friends at work, one attorney suggested to me that she thought it advisable to retain a top-notch attorney who was really familiar with criminal law. She proceeded to make the connection for me. When I met with him, he told me that he did not take private clients. However, since I came with a very high recommendation, he would listen to my tale of woe and said that he would get back to me in a week or so to let me know if he would take my case. While giving him my dissertation about the Baldinis and the police, he stopped me and said, "Let me tell you something."

I asked what that would be and he said, "I know all about the Baldinis, and I know about the corruption at the police department, and I believe you are on the wrong side of the political fence."

"And," I replied, "I am not a stupid woman. I do not need to pay you all this money for you to tell me this. I am paying you the money to do what needs to be done to protect my child from that evil."

We both knew where the other stood, and I left and went back to work.

Later that afternoon, apparently after he had checked out everything that I had shared with him, he called me and said, "It would be an honor to represent someone of your integrity and caliber!" I just knew in my heart that Jack Goodwinson was the answer to our prayers. It was an alliance cast down by the heavens.

I went to visit with my daughter later that evening and recounted everything that I had discussed with Jack. She seemed happy for the first time in a very long time. When we got home that evening, there was a message left on my answering machine, and I could not believe what I was hearing. It was a message from Olga. She was laughing into my phone and saying I was going to be very surprised to be hearing her voice.

She wanted to call me and tell me how sorry she felt for Melinda. She went on to tell me what a liar and snake that Stefan was and that he had real issues. As I tried to make sense out of what she was saying, I could not help but think to myself that she also had many issues and was a prolific liar. I stood there, right by the phone, screaming and crying with my body shaking uncontrollably. I could not believe that she would have the grit to call me after all that she and Stefan had done to us. I must have stood there for the better part of an hour; I was immobilized by the ghastly thoughts of her thinking that this would be amusing to all to have her call us. When I was finally able to compose myself, I went into my office and grabbed my dictator and made several copies of that message. I called all of the attorneys that both Melinda and I were involved with and told them what happened and brought them a copy of the taped message.

We were supposed to be in court for Michael's third pre-trial conference. We noticed that Stefan's van was at his house. It was late, and he was still at home. He drove away shortly thereafter, and we noticed that he was all dressed up. The conference had been continued, but apparently, he did not know that. They would let him sit there most of the day before they would tell him it had been postponed.

Melinda's primary attorney had been meeting with Melinda's probation officer, and they had also been meeting with Olga, the victim of the alleged crimes. The probation officer recounted how Olga was playing the victim role to the hilt. She cried and insisted that Melinda receive a minimum of one year in prison for what she had done to her. Melinda told me she was scared, and I told her that I was also scared.

We talked on the phone to Melinda regularly, usually several times a day, and we visited with her every visitation day without question. It was our routine. Sometimes we were lucky enough to have Melinda's child come with us. Stefan made us fight every step of the way in order to do that. Even though the visits had been court ordered, it was always at Stefan's whim. Sometimes he allowed it, and sometimes he did not. He was very good at making up excuses.

One day, Michael and I were going to pick the child up at the police station for a visit with his mother. When I drove past Stefan's house, he was outside in his driveway, and when he saw me, he immediately started giving me the finger in earnest and shouting his usual vulgarities. His mother's car was also in his driveway, and they were standing next to each other with the child when Stefan engaged in this juvenile behavior. I just kept driving to the police station and waited there for them to arrive. When his mother got to the police station, she was very insistent on handing me the child. It did not ring any bells at the time. I put him in my vehicle and drove off. She and Stefan were standing there laughing and laughing. When I got to the prison and I got the child out of his car seat, he could not walk. Every time I attempted to put him down, it seemed like he was in great pain. So I carried him.

When we got into the prison, he kept asking me to pick him up. I did, but he was very heavy for me to carry. All during the visit, he could not walk. I finally said to Melinda to take off his shoes and socks so I could get a look at his feet. Something was very wrong—a blister perhaps? When she pulled off his sneakers, his toes were twisted and contorted in an unusual manner.

When Melinda explored each of his sneakers, she pulled out a complete pair of socks from each sneaker that had been jammed down into the toe box. They did that to this little boy deliberately in order to get at me. How cruel. How painful that must have been for him. This was abusive.

It was nearly impossible for me to sleep at night, even though I was on much medication now. I slept for an hour and then I was up. There were so many thoughts running through my head. So many lies they had told and so many questions as to why and when this would all end. So much evil from one family!

Jack Goodwinson was our savior. He kept in constant communication with us. We met regularly, and he kept our morale high. He kept all of our other attorneys apprised of everything that was going on and made sure that anyone involved with Melinda was kept in the loop of information. Planning a winning strategy was one of his strongest qualities and sharing important information ran a close second.

We celebrated our twenty-fifth wedding anniversary in September in a very low-key manner—we tried to hide from everyone. We could not deal with anyone. However, our true friends would not let this momentous occasion pass without sending a card telling us they loved us, and that was a real joy for our hearts. Our true friends and wonderful neighbors knew the cross that we bore and understood. Their love was unconditional, very much like that of being a parent—unconditional!

Our little grandson had adapted to visitation with his mother quite well. He knew the routine, and it was all a game to him. His charm had won over the guard who facilitated the visits, and we considered him a friend. My grandson never failed to walk up to his friend at the end of a visit and shake his hand and say goodbye. And his friend always told him to be a good boy, and he always promised that he would. There was always some good to be found in every situation in life.

Just when we thought things had run their course and were getting better, there was always something that would slam us and take us down even farther than we had ever been. Melinda had been moved from maximum security to minimum, and that, for all concerned, was a good thing. It was so much less restrictive, and the family was allowed to bring in food and games, and visitation would be a whole lot easier with the little boy. However, because Stefan and his family had been calling child protective services complaining about an absent mother, they cited both parents for neglect, and the state had been involved in trying to place the child in state custody. The courts had decided that my husband and I were not fit grandparents and would not be allowed any further contact in order to take the child to visit with his mother. The state made this decision arbitrarily and based on no evidence and with no court hearing. The state now wanted Jim, the very man who lied to have Melinda incarcerated, to facilitate the visits.

It took every ounce of strength I had to not allow that to happen. That would have been like giving the fox entrance into the hen house to finish the job. I immediately sat down and wrote a letter to the chief judge of the family court and a copy to the chief judge of the Supreme Court. The letter contained all of my concerns about child protective services, their judges and their attorneys, and the impact it would have on this blameless child.

The court removed the worker from the case and offered an alternative option for visitation. I could elect to have Jim do the visits, or I could pay a state worker $150 per visit, and they would be permitted three visits per week. Money was now very scarce, but there was no question for me that I would choose the state worker.

I met with the state worker who would do the visits. She was an attorney at the courthouse. I gave her a check for the first visit and promised her that I would be there in person before each and every visit to pay her. She knew Melinda, and she eventually knew that I was trustworthy, and she would never have to think twice about receiving her money. She began to share special moments of the visits with me each time that I saw her. She had children that were close in age to my grandson, and she brought along some of their toys to the visits, and she told me what a wonderful mother Melinda was. It made my heart swell with pride. She told me about the condition of the child when the paternal grandparents dropped him off. The child was usually dirty, and his diaper was dripping from excessive urine. She saw what was going on here, but it was out of her control. She was a wonderful person and a source of consolation when we shared the events of a visit. My husband and I did not know if we would ever see the child again, and so every connection to him, however remote, was significant for us. My whole life was at the mercy of someone else.

We learned through the grapevine that our visitation was taken away from us because Stefan informed the protective services that I picked the child up at five p.m. on Friday evenings, and I would take him to the bars and hang out with him there. We were told by patrons of various bars, who happened to be friends of ours, that the state investigators had been going from bar to bar in our area with a picture of my grandson and I. They questioned patrons as to whether or not they have seen us in there. I thought to myself, *They were looking for me in drinking establishments?* How little they knew about me. I was picking my grandson up at the police station at five p.m. and driving to the prison for a six-to-eight p.m. visit with my daughter and returning him to the police station for eight thirty p.m. every Friday evening. The sign-in roster at the prison would have given a much better indication of where we were on any given Friday evening. I supposed they never thought to look for me in the churches or the monasteries and religious pilgrimages. That's where I spent a good deal of time, and I would take my grandson if the opportunity presented itself.

Michael's attorney came to our house, and preparation was all we had been doing for many hours now. We were preparing for Michael's criminal trial on Monday. Stefan's tenant and the tenant's daughter showed up as witnesses for the prosecution and were very insistent in speaking with Michael's attorney.

The attorney was very uncomfortable speaking with them without the prosecutor's presence to hear what they had to say. The prosecutor joined her, and the witnesses told them that they were there because Stefan asked them to lie for him, and payment would be in the way of free rent for a period of time.

The mother, being on ten years probation, felt trapped and forced into something she did not want to do. Both she and her daughter admitted that Michael had done nothing. He approached Stefan, wanted to speak with him man to man, but Stefan was on the telephone with the police.

Michael went over to the child, knelt down, cried, and told the child that he was sorry for not being able to keep his promise of taking him to visit with his mother and then down to our boat for the weekend. He got up and walked away. Most of the neighbors told the very same story to the police, who refused to listen to them or take a statement from anyone other than Stefan. Both attorneys thanked her and her daughter for telling the truth, and the prosecutor moved for dismissal. Another day, another hurdle completed.

My original restraining order against Stefan had expired, but Stefan's behavior continued and had escalated considerably. My neighbors were truly afraid for us and came to court to serve as witnesses in my new restraining order hearing. The sheriff came to my home about a week prior to this court appearance looking for Stefan to serve papers on him from child protective services. It was the same sheriff who had served me the papers from Olga. We both remembered our pleasant conversation from that situation, and she asked me how she could find Stefan.

I informed her, "We will be in court on the following Thursday, and I will be happy to call you and let you know when he arrives and you can serve him then." She was delighted! And, as a matter of fact, so was I.

As we waited in the hallway for the hearing to start, Stefan walked in with his friend, Slick. He sized us up and immediately got on his cell phone and called someone to give them a blow-by-blow description of what was happening. We heard him say, "Michael was making a phone call! and they were all high-fiving each other, and they were all laughing."

Before too much longer his mother came storming onto the scene, and she did not have a smile on her face. She looked gaunt. Shortly before we went into the courtroom, the sheriff served Stefan with papers that she had been unable to serve previously.

The trial began, and Stefan was pathetic. He was acting as his own attorney. His friend Slick reeked of alcohol and was also pathetic. These two did not agree on anything and did not address any of the issues at hand. The judge found Stefan to be unbelievable, and his witness to be absolutely incredible. The judge ordered a three-year restraining order, and Stefan was in

Louise Baron-Kent

disbelief that he did not win. The restraining order against Stefan was useless, though, as the police did not honor it. But it was a victory nonetheless.

Now that the case against Michael had been dismissed, we were doing battle with the department of corrections to get his visitation privileges restored. We tried at every visit to see if he would be permitted to visit with his daughter. And when it was a guard that we had come to know, they would let him in for a brief visit, and at other times he was outright turned away. We presented them with the dismissal papers from the courts. We went to the attorney general and got a criminal background check signed by the state, notarized, and with the official seal of the state. Nothing was good enough. It was very frustrating. It appeared that it was the job of the people of the state bureaucracy to give people as bad a time as they possibly could. I did not know what else they wanted from us.

It was nine days and counting until Melinda's release, and we were still fighting for visitation for Michael. We presented the guard with the official document with the raised state seal, and we were confident that we were a shoe-in. Not so; the guard did not believe that was an official document and threw it back at me and told Michael to get out. They were not even polite about it; they just enjoyed bullying so much. So he complied and sat in his truck so that I could visit. There was only one person in the whole corrections department who could authorize a document for visitation, and she did not work normal business hours, and she never returned phone calls, so that was the catch twenty-two. We had given up. It was not worth it. The next day would be eight days and counting.

A heavyset female correctional officer, who had witnessed the interaction between the facilitating guard and me, walked over to me and began to speak. I was sure she was going to accuse me of something and put me out too. She said in a gruff voice, "Let me see that document."

I knew that it was a genuine document, and I was not afraid to confront her. I handed her the paper, and she said to me, "This is an official document," and I responded, "Yes, it certainly is."

I said, "The facilitating guard wants me to come in and present this document to an officer who is never available. Further, it is not worth the bother because Melinda would be out on the first of the month, and by the time I finished jumping through all of the hoops and wasting countless time in jumping through those hoops, it is not worth the bother." Melinda's father would just wait in his vehicle and not see his child whom he had not seen since his arrest on July 2, and we would just play the game your way, as that was what made you all feel so good about yourselves.

About an hour into the visit, the female guard came over to me and told me I did not have to come back with any official document. She personally went into the computer and changed the status of Michael's visitation rights. She also informed me that if anyone had a problem with that, they could come and see her. She would take full responsibility. She told me to go out to the truck and get Michael so he could visit also. I wiped the tears from my eyes—*finally, a human being*. It was one tiny step after one tiny step after one tiny step. A constant battle, but victory was ever so sweet.

Four days before Melinda's release, she was having a visit with her child, and we were waiting outside for our visit with Melinda to begin. We noticed Erin and Jim desperately trying to see into the prison for a glimpse of Melinda in prison garb. Apparently, their life's goal was to witness their daughter-in-law suffering. They wanted to witness that for themselves with their own eyes.

Michael and I wanted to post Melinda's bail before she could be released on the first. That was an adventure all in itself. We made numerous telephone calls and visited the courthouse to try to figure out where we needed to be. The courts sent us to the department of corrections for women who, in turn, sent us back to the district court who, in turn, sent us to the men's prison, only to find out that bail could only be posted at certain times. We were told to be sure to bring the "handling fees."

Thieves! We went back at the specified time, only to find out we could not post bail until the day of release because it was on the first of the month and so on and so on. And the first would be a very busy day, so, in essence, pack a lunch.

It was October 31, Melinda's thirty-eighth birthday, Halloween, and the day before she would be released from prison. We had so much to celebrate. We brought a birthday cake to the visit, and we shared it with some of the other inmates. Nothing could ruin that birthday. We were full of hope and promise that the next day she would be a free woman once again. Life was not as we had planned for our child, but we believed that there was a purpose in all things.

Because the guard told us to come to the men's prison at ten a.m. to post bail, we were there with baited breath and a pocket full of money for the bail and "handling fees." We waited in line for an indeterminate amount of time, and when we reached the window, we were told to come back after two p.m. The guards laughed in our faces when they delivered their final indignation, but nothing would ruin our plans for that day. That was all about control and playing with vulnerable emotions. They intimidated us, and they loved it. It was such an adrenaline rush for them.

We returned to the men's prison shortly before two p.m., and we waited for hours in line for our turn. We carefully watched every person in line in front of us. There was some problem with everyone who presented to the window to pay his or her bail. The short, bald officer collecting the money took great delight in laughing and ridiculing everyone. It surely must have made him feel like a big man. When Michael and I arrived at the window, I made small talk with the officer about how busy they were. He returned the banter but had the last laugh as he handed us the receipt and told us, "You must now go and sit in front of the women's prison and wait for her release. I will call over to the women's prison and authorize the release only after a certain number of people had paid their dues and were processed." We were at their mercy, and he conveyed that message loud and clear.

An all-day adventure was what that turned out to be. We arrived at the prison in the morning as instructed, and it was now seven p.m., and we were still sitting in our vehicle and waiting. I went into the prison and spoke with the officer at the window and inquired as to whether or not Melinda was actually being released today. She telephoned down to the holding area and then told me that she was not anywhere near ready to be released yet. She was kind enough to take my cell phone number and said that she would call me with a heads up. I thought to myself, *Yeah, fat chance of that happening!* The guard told me that she did not have to do this, but she was just trying to help me out. I humbly thanked her for her kindness.

At seven thirty p.m., Melinda emerged from the prison. We all hugged and kissed and cried. It was a very happy reunion. Exhilaration would be a good description of the mood that was happening on the steps of the women's prison that evening.

Several days later we were at the family courthouse filing a motion to regain custody of Melinda's child. The hearing on the matter was set down for the following week because Melinda's attorney was on trial in another courthouse. As we were walking back to our vehicle, a short, heavy-set black woman grabbed my shoulder to say hello. I looked her in the eye, and I knew that I knew her, but I did not recall from where. She said, "I am the clerk who worked in the courtroom where the restraining order hearings were held."

All at once I recalled the prior exchanges that I had had with that woman. She inquired, "Are you here at the courthouse because you are still having problems with your son-in-law?"

I informed her, "I am here for moral support for Melinda, as my son-in-law has custody."

Her response to me was, "Please tell me he does not have custody of that child?"

"I am afraid he does," I replied.

And she, knowing Stefan from all of the restraining order hearings that she bore witness to, said, "Oh, God…no!"

I assured her, "We will keep on fighting."

We went to daycare and had a visit with the child, and he was so happy to see us both. He grabbed my finger and said, "Mema, come on. Let's go!" And then he grabbed his mother's finger, and he was ready to come with us. It broke our hearts when we had to say goodbye.

The Atonement

2008

On November 1 Melinda was released from prison for what would be her last incarceration, we hoped. She would remain on probation for another year and would be at the mercy of anyone and at risk of being re-incarcerated if anyone, known or unknown, filed a complaint with the courts saying that she was not acting in good character. There were no standards of proof to be met, and justice would be swift. She would be sent away. Stefan, his girlfriends, and family knew the system all too well, and we were sure they would try to break that maternal bond by concocting some story that would send Melinda back to prison. We had to remain even more vigilant than we had been previously. We did not trust anyone and kept her and her child within our view at all times.

Little Bryce had a doctor's appointment on Friday, December 12. I did not go with them, as I had some personal things to take care of that day. But at ten a.m. my telephone rang, and it was Melinda, and she was clearly shaken. When I asked her what was wrong, she told me that Olga had called her and needed to speak to her right away. She gave me Olga's cell phone number so that I could call her and see what she wanted. I could not even begin to imagine what that warped individual could possibly want, especially in light of there being a restraining order between the two.

Reluctantly, I called Olga at her restaurant so that I could determine if there was something I could help her with, and she said, upon picking up her cell phone, "Please do not hang up on me at any point during this conversation."

My head began to spin, and my breathing labored, and it took several seconds to comprehend what she was saying to me. She asked, "Can I meet with Melinda and you? I have some important things to say to you."

I informed her, "There is nothing that I want to hear from you."

She continued, "Stefan's mother was making big plans to have Melinda arrested again. In addition, Stefan himself was planning another event against Michael." I told her, "I need to sort this out in my mind, and I will get back to you."

I spoke with Melinda when she came home from the doctor's visit, and we discussed it both pro and con. Number one, it could be a trap because Olga had a restraining order against Melinda. Number two, she just might have something important to say, or number three, Stefan's family were using her once again in some way to hurt us further.

I called Michael, who was at work, and told him that we were inclined to go to see what that was all about. Michael was the dearest sweetest man ever. He was not an educated man, but he had more common sense than anyone I had ever met in my life. He said that we absolutely should not do a thing until we spoke with Melinda's attorney. However, he knew how thick headed I could be at times, and he begged me not to do a thing without benefit of input from the attorney. I called Melinda's attorney on the telephone and discussed the matter with her. She informed me that we were absolutely not allowed to go to meet with that woman unless she was present. So I said, "Well, then what are you doing this afternoon at four p.m.?"

And she responded, "I have a hairdresser's appointment, and I am desperate to get my roots done."

I said, "Well, if you are planning to be there with us, I guess you better reschedule your hair appointment!"

She said, "I will pick you up at your home shortly before four, and we will go to Olga's restaurant together." She advised, "Do not mention anything about me coming. I don't want to ruin that element of surprise."

I chuckled to myself that once she saw the attorney, that would be the end to any meeting. However, the attorney did not present any particular cause for alarm. In the meantime, I called Jack Goodwinson to inform him what had transpired, and he thought it was a good idea to meet with her, providing that we were not going in alone.

Once all of the groundwork had been laid, I called Olga back to set it up with her. Once she knew she had us coming, she began, "I want to apologize to you for all that I have done to your family. I feel awful and ashamed for what I have done. I don't sleep at night, and I can't eat. It just kept gnawing at me, and I am begging you for forgiveness."

I said, "For what you have done to Melinda and I, we have already forgiven you. This forgiveness is what has helped us to move forward in our lives. But what you have done to an innocent child, you need to look to a much higher power for that forgiveness." As far as I was concerned, what you do to deliberately hurt an innocent child and have him ripped away from his loving mother so that your boyfriend will like you more was unforgivable.

Melinda's attorney arrived at the appointed time, and we got into her vehicle and drove the three miles down the street to Olga's restaurant. We all sat in the car and talked generalities about what was going on, what could be expected, what our goal was in having this meeting, when Melinda announced that she had a tape recorder under her shirt. She was going to tape record that conversation. I was now a little nervous, the attorney was nervous also but weighed the legalities of taping the conversation and thought it was perfectly legal to do so and encouraged it.

We drove around to the back of the restaurant, as instructed by Olga. She had everything all planned out and did not want our vehicles to be parked out front in case either Stefan or his mother came by. She wanted to protect herself. She knew that Stefan was a volatile person, and if he knew that she was talking, he would think nothing of harming or trying to kill her.

Olga brought us inside via the back entrance and introduced us to her mother and sister, who worked in the restaurant with her. She strategically placed us at a table in the back of the room and out of view. She had Melinda sitting with her back facing the door and Melinda's attorney with her back facing the door. Olga and I were next to each other and faced the door. That way she could see who was coming in and take appropriate measures should Stefan or his mother stop by.

She stated, "I am really afraid of being caught because his family comes in here for fish and chips every Friday. And why not?" she explained. "They were free." So even when they were not speaking to one another, they never missed their free-standing order for Friday evening.

Once we were all seated and the introductions made and small talk that had dominated the conversation to lessen any tension had slowed, we got down to business. Melinda's attorney placed her cell phone on the table, as she did not want to miss the call she had been anticipating all afternoon.

Olga looked at it and announced, "I don't want to be tape recorded."

The attorney advised, "This is my cell phone," and handed it to her for inspection. I sat there straight-faced with a lump in my throat. Melinda was perfectly calm with a demure smile on her face.

Olga once again began to tell us that she was doing the meeting for herself. She admitted, "I lied on the stand under oath before the judge of the family court—horrible lies that had a profound affect on a young child's life, and I am having difficulty living with this now." She realized, "I can't go back to the family court to rectify those lies by telling the truth now because it would make me look like a fool." But on the other hand, what it was doing to her well-being was more than she could bear.

The attorney did not miss a beat in telling Olga, "Melinda has paid a very high price for all of the bad that you have done. Just imagine how Melinda feels, and imagine she has to live with this every day of her life. Just imagine how that must feel. But now, you, you who has instigated all of these atrocities, you want to feel better!"

The information that Olga was telling us was shocking, and it was hard to comprehend how individuals could conduct themselves and lie in such a prolific manner as to be believed by the courts. It was repugnant to think that someone would so deliberately and callously set out to annihilate a young woman and have no regard for the well-being of her young child.

We questioned her about things that she said to Melinda's probation officer, and Olga denied everything. So now we knew that she was lying yet again, and we could not help but wonder to ourselves if anything she said to us was true. She was a woman with a similar personality to Stefan's. Truth was not in their vocabulary, but yet she wanted to confess so that she could feel better about herself. It showed us the depths of her sickness and prolific evil of which she was capable.

Olga shifted the emphasis of the conversation to the divorce finalization and said, "You know what, Melinda? I don't think you got enough money in the settlement."

"As a matter of fact," I declared, "She got nothing. When one is married to a person like Stefan, one just wants it to be over—it is not about the money—it is not about anything but getting away from the abuse and to have the evils of Stefan, his mother, his family, and girlfriends out of our lives so that we can all move forward and rebuild."

She seemed sincere when she told Melinda's attorney, "I want to eliminate the restraining orders that we have between us."

The attorney informed her that she could take care of that easily enough for them both. Next week they would all appear before the judge of the superior court, and they would both testify that they no longer required restraining orders and that the orders should be vacated.

She continued on with her recounting and said, "Stefan has a new girlfriend now. Her name is Ellen. He lives there with her, and the child sleeps in the basement of her house, but I'm still dating him."

She knew full well that he was using her for his best interest by calling her and asking her to fabricate stories about Melinda to discredit her before the *guardian ad litem* that had been appointed to protect the best interest of the child.

He asked her specifically, "I need you to testify before the guardian and lie for me. Tell him that I don't live with Ellen and that his child is never with him when he is with Ellen."

And she willingly complied with his request. Olga seemed overly concerned with Stefan finding out about her telling us everything that had been going on and what was coming up for us.

We asked, "Why are you so afraid of Stefan?"

She claimed, "I am not afraid of him. I just don't want to put myself in harm's way."

She filled in the details of a neighborhood-wide restraining order being filed against Michael. Stefan paid a visit to every neighbor within a two-block radius of our home and tried to persuade everyone to come in and testify how awful Michael was. We had lived in that neighborhood for over forty years, and most of the older neighbors knew us really well and just laughed in his face. When he was not able to get neighbors to lie for him, he went to the local watering hole and paid several men of ill repute to lie for him.

She told us of how Stefan forged an alliance with Melinda's biological father and filled his head with really nasty information about Melinda. Melinda had never had a relationship with her biological father because he was abusive. He had always been abusive, and she did not want a relationship with her father, and it was her right to protect her child from any relationship. Olga told us that he kept that relationship going so that he could get information from the father. It was information that he could use against Melinda. It was the perfect opportunity for Melinda's father to get even with Melinda's mother for divorcing him some forty years prior. They were very similar personalities, and they got along famously. They were united in the devastation of Melinda and her family.

I asked Olga, "What on earth is it that you see in him? He never tells you the truth, and he uses you and encourages you to do dreadful things to people in order for him to satisfy his own ego."

She admitted, "I am a person with very low self-esteem, or no self-esteem for that matter, and I just need somebody. I am not particularly choosy who that is. Stefan was always available—for sex that is—and that was enough to keep me going back."

He took her no place, and they did nothing together, but because he paid attention to her in a quasi-romantic fashion, he was able to get her to do anything that he asked. It was unfathomable how someone could allow herself to be used like that.

When Olga came to the realization that he was playing both she and Ellen at the same time, she went over to Ellen's house late one evening and threatened her. The very next morning, Stefan went to the restaurant to punish her for going there. She said, "Ellen would not listen to me because she knows that I am a psycho! You better tell her that I am going to grab her by the throat the next time I see her, and then she can really see what a nutcase I am!"

What she was saying and her behavior scared me somewhat, and I realized that she was a very dangerous person.

I attempted to steer the conversation away from Olga and her interactions with Stefan's new girlfriend and back to the matter at hand. "What does Erin have planned? You said she had something big. What was she trying to do put Melinda back in jail?"

Apparently, no one in the family liked Olga; they looked at her like she was lacking in social etiquette or worse. But in any case, certainly not the type of person they would welcome into their family. They had never invited her to their homes, but they did call her from time to time to see how things were going, pretending to be concerned about her. They could not afford to let go of her because she was wacky enough to do whatever they asked her to do and whatever they were unable to do themselves. What Olga did not realize was that they had treated all of the women their son had associated with in any way, exactly the same way.

During one of their conversations, Erin said to Olga, "You know she's out of jail, and we need to do something… We are going to need whatever you have."

They were looking to Olga to come up with something once again that would put Melinda back in prison. "This was dangerous stuff. Why would you allow yourself to be used like that?" I asked.

Olga informed them, "Oh, no—no, no. Are you kidding me? If you want her in jail, you put her in jail yourself. I am not doing it anymore."

"I was so ashamed of myself. I could not tell you how horrible that I felt, and you may not believe me, but I felt awful. I felt really awful. My mother and I talked about it, and I promised her that I would call you and try to explain things. I could not even sleep at night. These crazy thoughts were always running through my head, and it was driving me crazy."

Melinda begged, "Tell me, Olga, why is it you were trying to have my mom, Michael, and me imprisoned for a year?"

Olga admitted, "If we worked in concert, we could pull off everyone being in prison for a lengthy period of time, then Stefan would get custody of the child, me and Stefan could get married and raise the child as our own. There would be no one left to fight for or care about the child."

Melinda was crying uncontrollably, and it was obvious that she was consumed with pain and fury. She began to scream at Olga, "Why did you make up these allegations? Why did you do this to me and my family? Why did you have me imprisoned and have my child taken away from me? How could you do this to another human being? How could you do this to a baby?"

And Olga replied, in a voice that was insincere, "I don't know. I guess it was because I was stupid. I was in love with Stefan, and I am a…liar…and I cannot make this up to you." Her answer was so cold and so matter of fact, it had no genuineness or remorse about it.

"No, you can't, and that pain that we all are feeling, especially Melinda, is going to be there for a long time to come," I managed to blurt out in an ever so soft voice. "You will never know the pain of a child saying to his mother as she is released from prison, 'Can I come home now, Mommy? Can I?' like he has done something wrong and he is being punished." He was a baby, and he had done nothing wrong, but he would be made to pay the price for a long, long time too.

Olga went on to tell us, "I never gave your child a second thought. It was your husband that I was interested in."

I told her, "This showed the kind of man Stefan really is."

Olga rephrased, "He is not a man."

I agreed that he was not. As far as I was concerned, he was not even human.

Melinda added, "He was a pitiful excuse for a human being. I couldn't believe that he would do everything that he had done to his own child."

The conversation then shifted to the incident when both Olga and Melinda showed up at the superior court house to file for restraining orders. I asked her, "Think back to the day when the mutual restraining orders were issued to both you and Melinda, and immediately thereafter, you filed a motion to adjudge Melinda in contempt. You stated in your complaint, 'Melinda was in the clerk's office and created a scene yelling at the court personnel that she wanted to see a damn judge now and that she was escorted from the courthouse'."

Just from the language used, I could tell these were Olga's words and nothing that Melinda would use. "You forgot, Olga, I was there with her and this did not happen." You also stated, "Melinda followed you from the courthouse to your car. She did not follow you. I was there. We were at least three hundred to four hundred feet behind you, and we were on the opposite side of the street. We were walking to Melinda's vehicle, which was parked on the main thoroughfare. You were parked on one of the side streets. And then you said Melinda took off all the lug nuts of your car and off your mother's car and put nails in your tires?"

Olga said, "Yeah, I know, but in my head these things were all happening. And when I talked to Stefan that day, he said it was you. Just like the incident with the three cigars in the gas tank, Stefan said you did this."

I said, "Do you know the amount of strength that it would take to get all of the lug nuts off of your vehicle? There was no way any female could do that without impact wrenches, but if you did manage to muster that incredible strength to get them off, there was one nut on every tire of the newer vehicles that required a 'key' to get it off. This special tool would be in the glove compartment of your locked vehicle."

She declared, "I know that now, but Stefan told me it was Melinda."

I personally did not believe any of that happened, and I did not believe many things that she was saying to us. It was more that Stefan told her to file the report and she fabricated the story.

She continued to tell us about the incident that resulted in one of the three arrest warrants issued against Melinda, which occurred on the morning of August 17 at five a.m., wherein she stated to the police that Melinda came at her with her cell phone taking pictures of her while swinging both fists at her.

I asked her, "How would that be possible since a cell phone camera does not have a light source? It was quite dark at five in the morning, and if both your fists were in the air and swinging, how would it be possible to take a picture?"

She said, I don't know, but Stefan told me this was the way it happened."

I was convinced she could not think for herself. Everything that she thought or said was what someone else had said to her. She was truly a desperate woman. She continued even further by stating, "I didn't show up for the contempt hearing because I was already successful in getting Melinda incarcerated with my story about the courthouse incident."

As Olga continued on with her story about Stefan and his family, I could not help looking at her and feeling sorry for such a wretch. I could not help but stare at her and wonder if she was really telling the truth. If she was, why would anyone let someone use them like that in such a danger filled life style and all at her expense? She was truly pathetic.

When she told us that Stefan thought every woman was in love with him and that he was something really special, I knew that to be true. We discovered for ourselves that Melinda was not the first person that he had done these things to. There have been a long string of women from Alabama to California with broken hearts and empty bank accounts.

Olga said, "I really loved him, and that is why I did the things I did for him, but he is a violent person, and I almost stabbed him on a couple of occasions during domestic squabbles."

She readily admitted, "I told nothing but lies to the judge during the family court divorce hearings because that is what Stefan wanted and asked me to do for him. He boasted about what he had done to his wife and told everyone he only married Melinda because she had money and land."

Melinda acknowledged, "This is the truth. He admitted that to me shortly after the marriage, and he had worked very diligently to get it all away from me. The money was all gone, but the land remained."

Melinda was very sad when she told Olga, "Stefan would not have been able to take my child from me unless he was successful in having me incarcerated and you played right along with him with your lies. You had no concern for anyone but yourself."

I told Olga, "You better watch out for yourself, because Stefan and his family may make every attempt to have you put in jail once all was said and done."

Olga told us, "He better watch out for me, because I will take the knife!'"

I was now internalizing that these were not normal people—these were very sick and demented people! I could see the horror associated with these deviants, and it made me very uncomfortable.

Michael and I knew for a fact that they were both violent with each other. One evening as we were heading upstairs to the bedroom, we looked out the window on the stairway and looked in the direction of Stefan's house. We saw Olga's vehicle in his driveway, and the light illuminated the bay window in the kitchen. We could see everything happening in the kitchen. We saw Stefan go to the kitchen door and open it, and in walked Olga. Before long they were fist fighting with each other. We couldn't believe our eyes, so we got out the binoculars and watched the scenario unfold. Melinda's attorney asked, "Did you call the police?"

I replied, "Hell no. We were down on our knees praying that one of them would kill the other that night and solve all of our problems." That fighting went on for a good half an hour before all the lights went out and it got quiet. Her vehicle was still parked there in the morning, so we thought in retrospect that the fight must have been the foreplay before the sex!

Olga claimed to be remorseful for allowing Stefan to control her and that she had difficulty being with herself because of all the bad she had done. She had been a liar all of her life and had no use for people. She connected with Stefan because they enjoyed the same things and were similar people.

Melinda was validated by all that she had heard from Olga. She often thought that perhaps she was going crazy by his victimizations and brutality. But now, she could see it very clearly for what it was. Other women were now enduring his wrath. She collected all the vague pieces of information that Olga offered, and she was able to put them all together and into proper perspective and see the big picture and knew that she

Louise Baron-Kent

was not imagining things. Olga's mother joined the conversation and told Melinda, "There is something wrong with that guy—he is nuts." Her mother told us, "I find my daughter disgusting for what she has done."

Olga was sickened by the fact that Stefan had custody of the child and believed he was in a bad environment. She was hopeful that these ninety-six minutes of true confession would allow her to feel better about herself. In my estimation, by telling us all of the bad things she had done, how she had impacted everyone's existence in such a negative way, and the life altering effects it would have on the small child, it was not enough contrition to obliterate a guilty conscience and make her feel good about herself. I could not feel any sincerity of remorse in anything that she had said.

When the meeting had concluded, we all breathed a sigh of relief, and we all superficially hugged and thanked each other. When we exited through the back door of the restaurant, Olga pulled Melinda aside and said, "If you ever want to get together sometime, please call me."

They hugged once again, and Melinda got into the car. Melinda's attorney noticed that it was very quiet in the back seat and asked, "Are you okay, Melinda?"

Melinda was crying and could not answer. That meeting had been very traumatic for her. Melinda felt used, and her attorney assured her that she was not the first one and there would be others. No one spoke on the short ride home.

I spent every free and waking moment of the next three weeks transcribing that recording into a typed and easily readable transcript of what had happened at that meeting. The digital tape recorder was sent to a forensic audiologist for authentication, duplication, and packaging as evidence, and a chain of custody was established. The copies and transcripts were forwarded to Jack Goodwinson for possible use as evidence to discredit and impeach the testimony of Olga at the time of Melinda's appeal in the superior court.

The Revelation

2008

When so many bad things happen to one person or in one family, with no end in sight, the natural progression of things would be to explore the reasons why. On more than one occasion, we had both individually and collectively as a family turned our thoughts inward to investigate our own being to determine if our perception of the world was somehow flawed. Or perhaps our expectations of human behaviors were too high. The questioning of self was never ending. However, it was beyond our comprehension that we had all led admirable lives, had been productive and contributing members of society all of our lives, and then, one day, we awoke, and the entire family was suddenly all criminals. All of this having only taken place since Melinda's marriage to Stefan. It didn't make any sense to us. Something was very wrong, and we needed to figure out how that could be fixed. I believed our operative word was *Stefan*. There just did not seem to be any help for us. Bad things just kept happening, and there did not appear to be any way for us to protect ourselves from what was happening to us.

Watching television had never really been a great form of entertainment in my life. Sometimes it offered good educational information and surely was worthwhile, but I was a person who worked hard. I enjoyed and preferred being out helping my neighbors, working on projects around my home, taking care of my family, interacting with friends, and maintaining good positive energy to accomplish until day was done. That was what kept me going. Though, in the last several years, my activity levels had changed dramatically. One evening in the summer of 2009, my husband was acting remote and was apparently at a low point and needed me to just come and sit by him while he watched some television to take his mind off things. It made him feel better just having me there next to him.

After a short time of consoling him, reassuring him, and just being there for him, he felt more at ease and decided to go upstairs to bed. It was as if there was some sort of divine intervention taking place. He drew me to the television, which I ordinarily would not have partaken in. He was watching a documentary about a world-famous doctor, a psychologist. He had developed a "scale" of different levels of psychopathy. He explained the different levels and what the characteristics of the different levels were and how they manifested themselves. That program was so compelling that I could not bring myself to walk away from it. I became obsessed, and I wanted to know more, as much as I could possibly learn. Everything this doctor was talking about described Stefan. That television program opened my

Louise Baron-Kent

eyes to what was really going on with him. It was the catalyst for intense research on my part.

When the program finished, I was sitting on the couch crying. I thought or at least I perceived them as tears of joy, because I had been pounding and pounding on a door that would not open, and suddenly on the last pound—*bam!*—it opened, and things suddenly became crystal clear.

By now it was late, and I had to go to work the next morning, but I was compelled, uncontrollably so, to stay sitting there on that couch and observe. I was being held captive by some indescribable force. The next program to come on was another documentary about the family court system in the state of New York. I was mesmerized and held captive by my own fears of what was happening to us personally as I was compelled to watch. The story I witnessed that evening brought more tears of horror and disbelief. It was the same scenario that we were facing here in our own state in the family court.

It was only after these two television programs and a good healthy cry that I realized that if these abuses of power were going on in New York, then there was a good possibility that it was not isolated to that one state. These two programs that I was drawn to were the catalyst that moved me in the direction of endless research about corruption in my own state's family court system and the science of psychopathy. I was like a madwoman in my quest, and the results left me reeling in disbelief.

My disbelief in the fact that we were in the United States of America and we had a Constitution that protected us and kept bad things from happening to good people and that corruption was not possible. We had state laws and rules of procedure in our court systems that were in place for the protection against any wrongdoing. I was under the impression that there was equality and justice for all, or so I thought. But, as I was finding out, all was not as it appeared.

My research showed me that someone with the dysfunction of psychopathy often was described as charming, witty, and immediately likeable. When I read just these few words and thought about their meaning and their correlation to our situation, it was as if an explosion took place in my head. These words immediately brought to mind the day that we first met Stefan. When Melinda first introduced the love of her life to us, he was so charming and soft spoken and quite demure as he fell all over Melinda, tending to her needs. He told us, "Now that I'm going to be a part of your family, I can do so much for you and help you with chores that need to be done around your property."

We were smitten; he seemed too good to be true. We were falling in love too, and we were so happy for Melinda. It is also quite true that a psychopath overpowers with flattery, and one never even realizes it until it's too late. They exuded confidence and a desire to be liked by all. As time went on and the relationship developed, Stefan was always around us, he helped us with whatever we needed to get done and even worked on projects that he created on his own. He displayed such cockiness and a reassuring persona that we were ingratiated for everything he was doing on our behalf. We truly believed that he was the most wonderful person on earth. I even jokingly said to Stefan's mother on several occasions, "When you don't want him anymore, I will adopt him!" I personally believed a psychopath to be a bad person, someone who would be easily identifiable as a person of not good character. The truth of the matter was that someone could be standing right next to you, and you would not have a clue that there was anything wrong. One could even be a doctor or a lawyer or the person living right next door.

Louise Baron-Kent

Only with time and close observation along with much trepidation was an individual exposed for their true identity. Psychopathic personalities were highly impulsive and had a hardened disregard for others. In other words, they had no conscience, remorse, or sense of guilt. They were self-serving. The more I researched and studied, the more easily I could identify many of the character traits of a psychopath in Stefan and related them to the behaviors I had seen from him. Stefan's behaviors were very transparent from the very beginning. If we had only listened to our guts instead of our hearts from the outset, perhaps there would be no need to be telling this story.

Though there always was that fear, such as we had from the very beginning, that it would be wrong to rush to judgment. Stefan loved to spend his entire paycheck indulging himself in new tools that he not only did not need but that he already had several of. There was no end to his wanting, and there was absolutely no thought to anyone having to do without so that he could have. He believed he was entitled.

And then, of course, there was the time that Stefan convinced Melinda that he needed an ATV so that he could use it doing yard work. He saw the ATV listed on the Internet for five thousand dollars cash, American money. He went to Melinda's bank and got a money order out of her bank account and sent it to a company in Italy that was supposed to deliver it the next day Federal Express. I tried to tell him something was not making sense here. This was a big item, and there was no way this could come from a foreign country in a day. It turned out to be a scam, but Stefan was unconcerned, after all, it was not his money that he used. We, for the first time, began having second thoughts about Stefan.

without providence

193

Often psychopaths are superficially caring of others or charming but very into themselves, egocentric, if you would. When we first met Stefan, we actually fell in love with him. Stefan had such a way of talking you into wanting to be with him. He was always doing things for us and for the neighbors in order to be more attractive to them. Some of the neighbors who Stefan had done free electrical work or construction work for and who were ingratiated to him, were then asked to return the favors by lying for him in a court of law. They willingly did so. For a period of time, we thought he was the next best thing to sliced bread. His constant motion and always having to do something, some project, was an indication to us at the time that he was very industrious. He was always busy, and it was clearly viewed by us, unsuspecting individuals, as being ambitious. Little did we know that this constant motion and having to do something at all times was not a good thing. Psychopaths were bored easily. We could now identify that trait, but it was way too late for that.

When we stopped to think of all the times that he acted in an irresponsible manner, we could see how he squandered Melinda's money. It was necessary for him to constantly and continually reward himself with objects and non-essentials. However, when he was angry with Melinda, he would smash and destroy only those possessions that belonged to her. His behavior certainly tended toward the traits of acting impulsively and recklessly, and he took no responsibility for any of his actions.

When Stefan and I did work on projects together, he shared much of his past with me, and I never for a moment considered him a psychopath, because I did not know what psychopathy was all about. I had no need to know about this sickness. Ignorance was truly bliss at this point in time. For the most part, no one ever wakes up in the morning and thinks to himself, *I think I will welcome a psychopath into my home today!* No one ever thinks about the malady unless there is some reason to think about it. When he told me about all of the short-term relationships he previously had prior to marrying Melinda, I chalked it up to the normal male ego. His claim to fame was that he had bedded over fifteen hundred women in his short life. I thought that incredible and perhaps even impossible. But, after knowing him and seeing his behaviors, I now had come to realize that this was possible with him. Stefan, even during his marriage, always had a couple of girlfriends and never thought much about his actions. He hid this fact from Melinda quite well until after Bryce was born, but from that point forward, he found no need to conceal his actions any longer.

As time went on, we realized that Stefan acted with emotional deficiency, and he merely mimicked behaviors he had previously seen. He did not really know how to act with others. He commenced friendships in order to use people to his best advantage.

When he was no longer in need of whatever a friendship provided to him, the friendship was over, or at the very least, fell by the wayside.

Stefan's grandiose sense of self and his propensity for always lying to everyone and manipulating and conning manifested itself into having his wife arrested on numerous occasions for crimes that were clearly concocted in his head. However, he was the master manipulator. He knew exactly what to say and how to act to get everyone to believe him. He clearly used his abilities for self-serving purposes. He decided when they divorced that he would leave his wife praying for and welcoming death over the existence that he would leave her. His lack of remorse over his deep-seated rage at his wife was contrary to any human being we had ever encountered. The brutality, the physical and mental abuse he inflicted on her, were abnormal by any stretch of the imagination. He never, at any point, felt or showed any guilt for his actions, and to him the end always justified the means. He truly did not know what love was all about. It was always about him and him alone.

His ability to impose rage and vilify his wife and her family were often accompanied by some little expression of feigned regret. That created the enabling of an addictive circularity for all involved in their relationship. He truly lived a parasitic lifestyle by taking from his wife and using for himself. The more I studied this mental defect, the more I was able to understand Stefan's behavior. People who were psychopathic were not candidates for any therapeutic intervention. There was no way that these people could be cured or made whole. Inflicting pain on others was gratifying to them. Every time Stefan had his wife arrested by either himself or by having his girlfriend fabricate some story, when the arrest occurred, Stefan was always in close proximity to the arrest, and he always became animated with excitement. That was his life, and he enjoyed it so much. We can, in retrospect, see how he manipulated his attorney into believing that he was the innocent party; his wife was the crazy person. Because of this belief by the attorney, he dictated his orders to the police in a clear and convincing manner to impart the fact that we are the bad people. He furthered the complicity through the attorney's wife, who aided her husband in his endeavor to produce for his client through her position at the Attorney General's Office. Psychopaths are masters of manipulation and deceit.

Neither Stefan, Erin, nor Kathy believed that there was anything wrong with Stefan. They believed his behaviors to be perfectly normal. Which, of course, begged the question, "Do they really believe this?" Or were they in denial and trying desperately to normalize him? And if neither of these were true, then there was a good possibility of him having grown up in a psychopathic "family" where lying, lack of emotion, superficial charm, manipulation, being above the law with a grandiose sense of self, parasitic behavior, shallowness, needing constant stimulation, boredom, promiscuity, juvenile behavior, irresponsibility, and a lack of boundaries were their way of life. I was fairly certain in my convictions that the latter would be true for the entire family. We thought back to the Thanksgiving Day greetings and could very clearly see the lack of boundaries in that family.

With each passing day, the bits and pieces of information that I had gleaned on psychopathy played over and over in my head and easily took me back to a multitude of instances that had occurred. I reflected on a characteristic, and my mind immediately took me back to a specific instance and provoked much internal anxiety, as I could not help but wonder how we could have missed all that had happened. The red flags were all there, and the behaviors were so obvious, but yet, seemed perfectly normal, until one actually studied the condition. I prided myself on being a good judge of character and not easily deceived into accepting an individual who was so harmful to peaceful coexistence of families. I had been humbled.

My mind readily drifted back in time to the courtship phase of the relationship when we celebrated Thanksgiving and Christmas with Stefan's family. Things that I discounted as pre-wedding nervousness on the part of his mother, who became quite agitated with me for having brought a dessert to the gathering—red flag. Erin, who actually had no friends, had such grandiose feelings of self, believed everyone wanted to be with her, especially after her success of luring away a man from a thirty-eight-year marriage. "Come and look at my prize, my trophy." She was not about to endure another woman stealing her thunder by bringing a dessert, especially when the praise was coming from her husband.

The way the men in the family greeted the sister by kissing her up and down her neck and touching her body in inappropriate places—red flag. We subsequently learned that Stefan and his sister Kathy were as children and in all probability still are lovers. Erin was always away snatching other women's husbands. Stefan's eagerness to tell all about this woman he knew or that woman he knew, falsely believing that all women were in love with him plainly demonstrated behaviors he had seen from his mother. Male psychopaths believe that all women lust after them. They are so virile and masculine that women just fall under their spell and instinctively want to be a part of their life. His phony charm and demure persona played right into this belief of animal magnetism. Once the relationship was over with any of these women that he had seduced, he threw them away like they were garbage because he was no longer interested; however, he was compelled to do awful things to them for their audacity to believe that he would actually seriously be in love with them.

Stefan's wanting his wife to put all of her assets in his name and/or jointly held—red flag. He had to keep accumulating wealth by deceptive means from women because he spent money with reckless abandon. Stefan was very selective of any woman he was seriously involved with. The serious contenders had to possess substantial financial means and assets. Once he had worked his magic, Stefan was then the proud owner of all the assets, and the female was left destitute and ashamed. Stefan had done this many times.

Louise Baron-Kent

Always calling the police at a whim and his abnormally high opinion of himself—red flag. Because of the relationship between himself and his attorney and the attorney's wife and the Attorney General, Stefan thinks nothing of calling 911 and filing false reports with the police, whether it be about us, or others, he was not discriminatory. He had the upper hand. He calls the police and they come immediately. There is no questioning, there is no need for probable cause, there was only Stefan's word and an arrest coupled with tens of thousands of dollars to defend against what he had said. We had been conditioned. We would not call the police for anything, not even if we were being attacked by a knife-wielding intruder.

His inability to control his behavior and impulsivity let Stefan act in any way he chose and whenever he chose. Stefan did what he wanted when he wanted. He had no boundaries, and his psycopathy escalated with each and every year. Some day, the unthinkable just might happen to him when he pushes the wrong person too far.

The one behavior that I sincerely believed should have been a red flag, easily identifiable to anyone, was the fact that he had lived in so many places throughout the country, and he never stayed in one place for very long. He was unable to hold down a job. He did not ever take responsibility for the loss of employment and convinced everyone that the terminations were always someone else's fault. This ordinarily would make anyone suspicious, but when you had not known someone for very long, it was so easy to overlook and explain away. There were so many instances. This list could go on and on and on. However, identifying these characteristics through hindsight did not do anyone any good. It was hard not to blame ourselves for not knowing.

But, when looked at realistically, it would have been impossible for anyone to know.

While investigating this malady, I discovered that there was evidence suggestive of genetic influences that lent themselves to propagating a psychopathic personality, as the brain did not process information in the same manner as someone without this dysfunction. It was widely believed that this condition became distinct at a very early age and evolved into permanency by the teen years. A dysfunctional environment, together with other social forces, usually suggested a strong basis for developing these maladaptive behaviors. Sometimes attempts at therapeutic intervention could create a more profound intensity for acting out the grandiose ideas.

It infuriated me to no end to know that a relationship that was so full of promise and our belief that the union was a marriage made in heaven was truly a relationship based on a distorted understanding that could not withstand the test of time. It became a relationship full of broken promises, deceit, and betrayal. While the control that Stefan had over us was quite rewarding and gratifying to him, the aftermath for our family had cost us our lives. It had cost us hundreds of thousands of dollars to defend ourselves in the community and in the judicial system. Our reputations as caring and understanding human beings had been tarnished. We no longer had any protection from our police department, and for a long period of time, our lives were not worth living.

It never ceased to amaze me how easily we were all fooled and how unconstrained Stefan was in his efforts to destroy a good family. He had never given our lives or our well-being a second thought. We were nothing more than obstacles to be overcome and eliminated accordingly. It was all a game, a game that Stefan enjoyed playing. The really scary dilemma for us was that he now had custody and placement of our grandchild—a child who he would now be able to mold in his own image, a child still in the formative years—and the courts had given him *carte blanche* to raise and influence. Just the thought made all of us bristle with anger.

During the continuing process of the family court proceedings a *guardian ad litem* was appointed to act in the best interest of the child. His role as the guardian was to interview all persons involved in the child's life and make life-altering decisions for the child based on his findings. The guardian was responsible for consistently acting in the best interest of the child and to advocate for the child. He was to understand and uphold the law, as it pertained to his appointment, and be always cognizant of the law to maintain the highest of standards of professionalism and cultural sensitivity and have the highest degree of ethics. He was to conduct, plan, document, and complete a thorough, appropriate, and fair investigation of the facts and make recommendations communicated to the court in a timely fashion.

The guardian appointed to Bryce conducted his investigation of the father and the father's family and decided that the father would have custody without the benefit of seeking out other court records to ascertain why Melinda had been imprisoned so many times. He spoke with Melinda for several minutes, and, on one other occasion, he spoke with the child for several minutes. That was the entire extent of his investigation. In his bill, he noted the numerous conversations with Erin and other members of Stefan's family and his girlfriends. The investigation was one sided and biased. He denied visitation to Melinda based on no facts whatsoever. He made life-altering decisions for the child without information or forethought.

In a lengthy correspondence to the guardian, I outlined his inappropriate behavior, poor decision-making, and inability to act in the best interest of the child. I called his attention to the way we had seen Stefan behave and interact with people in his everyday life. I had made a great effort to research pyschopathy, not only for our benefit, but also for the benefit of the guardian, so that he could make an informed decision for the child.

I wanted him to know that these people were grandiose with a sense of entitlement; they were pathological liars who deceived, cheated, and manipulated; they lacked empathy and remorse. They did not develop deep emotional and/or social connections with others and exploit without regret. They displayed superficial charm, led parasitic lifestyles, displayed promiscuous sexual behaviors, and were capable of only short-term relationships. They were impulsive, had poor behavioral controls, and failed to accept responsibility for their own actions. They were self-absorbed and egocentric, lacked respect for the law, lacked inhibitions, behaved inappropriately, and had no shame.

I informed him that he had considerable interactions with Stefan according to his own report. I implored him to really see what was going on. This child should not be in this sort of environment. But he, as an educated professional, would not open his eyes. No amount of research conducted by other educated professionals would influence his authority.

I went on and begged him for psychological testing for both parties before any final decisions were made. I pushed for the testing repeatedly, and the court and the guardian finally relented. Because Melinda had been involved with the family courts through her employment for the state, it was virtually impossible to obtain an impartial psychologist to perform this testing. The judge's opinion was, "Just get anyone. It's not important anyway!" In other words, they were going to do the testing only to appease my verve. This is our family court system at its finest. We have judges who get bored with a case and take the day off or show their boredom by making such a callous statement to "just get anyone." Judges in this state are appointed for life, and there is no need for them to be overly concerned with anything.

Eventually a psychologist with a ten-year history with Melinda was retained to conduct the testing. This in my estimation was unquestionably a conflict of interest. However, we were not given any choice if we insisted on proceeding. The testing was conducted in the summer. It consisted of one short interview each, the testing, and the final report.

On the day that the report was to be entered into the court records, each party was allowed to peruse a ten-page report for approximately ten minutes. It was impossible to read this lengthy report within the time frame allowed, never mind attempt to digest the information and wrap our minds around what it was referring to. However, the bottom line was that Stefan, the report confirmed, was a psychopath, and Melinda was declared to be untrusting and therefore abnormal. However, it was my belief that if the psychologist had bothered to elicit from Melinda all of the abuse she had endured and the number of times that her former husband had concocted stories, had her arrested and incarcerated, he could have easily discovered why Melinda was untrusting. That was never explored. The judge never read the report and ordered it sealed in the court records, never to be seen again.

October 6, 2009, was the day for taking the testimony of the psychologist and the day the attorneys would have been able to challenge the report and its methods, raw data, interview rationale, etc., of the psychologist and/or testing services utilized by the psychologist. Neither attorney questioned any element of the testing. Nor did they question the psychologist in any manner. Had they bothered to do so, they would have discovered that the test administered to Melinda was inappropriate because she suffered from PTSD and severe depression. The test administered was contrary to standard operating methods used for individuals with such conditions, and, therefore, the outcome was severely flawed.

It was forever etched in my mind when the psychologist got up on the witness stand and the judge asked him for a diagnosis of Stefan. The psychologist proceeded to tell the judge that, "Stefan bears all the characteristics of a psychopath and proceeded to elaborate further that someone with this condition will not benefit from therapeutic intervention." He then proceeded to a diagnosis of Melinda. He stated that, "Melinda has low self-esteem and is untrusting of people."

The judge looked him square in the eyes and said to him, "So they were both the same?"

The psychologist said, "No! There may be some similarities, but they are not the same."

The judge pierced his look down on the psychologist and said, "So they *are* the same?"

The psychologist recognizing the anger in the judge's voice said shakily, "Yes, as you say, they are both the same!"

The judge proceeded to question the psychologist further as to whether he would be willing to do post-divorce couples' counseling.

The psychologist said, "I don't ordinarily get involved in situations like that, but if that were what the judge was ordering, I would be happy to comply." This statement was made just minutes after he already testified to the fact that someone with Stefan's condition and level of dysfunction would not benefit from therapeutic intervention of any kind.

The clarity of the game that was being played out there was very reminiscent of the television programs that I had stumbled upon and the research that I had completed in anticipation of this day in court. It was a big game, and everyone except the parties involved would profit at the expense of a child.

The Calm Before
the Storm

The Holidays 2008

Melinda was a free woman. We needed to stay focused on the appeal, and she needed to fulfill her probation requirements. We kept her very close to the vest. She was not allowed out of our sight until she was truly free. Through my friends and acquaintances, Melinda and I both met some wonderful people who were all willing to help out in any way they could by offering small amounts of money, a place to stay, food, and encouragement. The generosity of strangers was overwhelming. It was only in a time of such great need, such as ours, did we really come to understand and appreciate the value of family and friends.

We stayed close to family and friends as much as we could so that neither Stefan, his family, nor his girlfriends would be able to make up anything else to take Melinda away from her son ever again. We would always have someone who could and would confirm our whereabouts. Realistically, it was not a fun way to have to live life, but when we thought of the alternative, it was only for a year and was doable as far as we were concerned.

It was amazing how our network of friends grew from one person to so many caring people who welcomed us warmly. We felt such a true sense of caring and goodness, which was refreshing and heartwarming.

Now that Melinda was out of prison and terminated from her employment just as Erin had so diligently worked toward, they requested that she come to pack up her belongings and personal possessions and remove them from her office. Michael went with her to collect her items, and she walked out of there with her head held high for the thirteen years of admirable service that she provided to the children of the state that she so deeply cared for and their families. She knew in her heart that she did a great job, no matter what anyone else may have thought. Michael even accompanied her to every probation meeting and informed the probation officer that she was never alone and he would not let her go through this alone either.

Because Melinda had not seen her child officially since being released from prison, she made a special plea to the court for visitation. They made arrangements for her to have a supervised visit with a social worker at the child protective service unit. It was more humiliating for her than being in prison. She packed up his little wheelie suitcase with juice boxes, and Michael made him some Jell-O, and the girl at the attorney's office packed a little bag with candy for him and brought an assortment of his toys. When he spotted his little suitcase, he squealed and jumped for joy. It was his, and his mom could not be far behind. She was allowed fifty minutes with her child, and when the visit was over, the social worker opened the door and told Melinda in a brusque voice to get out. No amount of humiliation would have kept her from seeing her child.

Before Melinda had been released from prison, she asked me, "Mom, please go to the courthouse to determine if there are any fines that I owe and please get them out of the way so that we don't have to waste time after I'm released, or that will prevent me from gaining freedom altogether." Michael and I went to the courthouse to gather information and clear up any impediments to freedom.

A thin, black woman informed me how to go about posting bail and acknowledged to me that no fines existed because her case was on appeal. She also told me, "Don't forget the hearing on November 19."

I inquisitively responded, "Hearing on the nineteenth? No one has been notified of any hearing on the nineteenth!"

She looked at me and smiled and said, "Listen to what I am telling you! Do not miss this hearing on the nineteenth."

Once again, I replied, "No one knows anything about any hearing on the nineteenth."

She looked at me square in the face, and her eyes grew large, and her brow rose very high on her forehead, and a sinister smile erupted on her face, she once again said, "Listen to what I am telling you. Do not miss the hearing on the nineteenth!"

With the look that she gave me and the words that she used, I came to the realization that, number one, no one knew about that hearing, and, number two, if we missed it, we were all done.

I immediately got on the phone and called Jack Goodwinson. He informed me that there was no such hearing on the nineteenth. A call to Melinda's other attorney elicited the same response. Repeated efforts evoked the same response each time. I took the bull by the horns and asked them both to humor me and be in court on that date.

I thank the Lord each and every day that I was led to that courthouse and found out about that hearing. If not for that, Melinda would not have shown up, and a new warrant would have issued for her arrest, and she would be put back in prison. We all showed up to the infamous non-hearing. Melinda did not wear any jewelry, nor did she have any personal possessions with her because she feared for the worse. She went before the judge, and he, after much consternation, was merciful. The attorney general wanted Melinda incarcerated for another ninety days because she had not complied with the sentencing requirements that she seek out an "in-patient" mental hospital confinement upon release. The judge flat-out refused.

The assistant attorney general subsequently begged, "Please sentence Melinda to home confinement for the remainder of her sentence."

The probation representative objected and came to Melinda's defense and affirmed, "There is no in-patient residential treatment for someone who was depressed and/or suffered from post-traumatic stress disorder to comply with those sentencing requirements."

The probation representative went on to tell the judge, "Melinda is very cooperative and has been involved in an outpatient treatment program and other spiritual endeavors."

Jack Goodwinson presented the judge with numerous letters personally prepared by neighbors, friends, mental health professionals, and spiritual directors, who deemed it important to vouch for the character of this wonderful woman and beg the courts to show mercy. God bless each and every one of them.

The judge read only two, one from Melinda:

If I were free today, I would drop to my knees and thank God for being merciful and allowing me a new beginning to my life. I would grab hold of my son, Bryce, who is only two years old, and I would hug him and kiss him and tell him how sorry I am that I was not able to be in his life for a brief period of time because of circumstances beyond my control. I would promise him that I would be the best mother that I could be to him and that we would live "rich," not in money and toys and all the worldly trappings that one thinks of when one thinks of the word *rich*, but rich in spirit and hope and of sharing whatever time that we were together, from this day forward. And I would hug and thank my parents, who have always believed in me and have stood by me through this whole ugly process, and tell them how lucky I am to have them in my life and beg them for forgiveness for all that they have had to endure financially, physically, and emotionally. I would thank them for the most precious gift of all—their time. They worked tirelessly to be there for me and help me to be strong to get through this ordeal. I would work diligently toward finalizing my divorce and move forward with my life in a positive direction, and I would move to a "safe house" so that neither my soon-to-be ex-husband nor any of his girlfriends know where I am, and I would never again fall victim to the "violation of probation" dilemma.

I lived the last several years as a battered and abused spouse, and because of that, I am severely depressed. My goal is to continue on my medication and seek counseling, either outpatient or perhaps more intensive therapy as an inpatient. It is important that I work on getting me well, as I believe that is the key to leading a productive life in the community.

Once I am well and emotionally stable and feeling good about myself, I would begin the process of reinventing myself—find my place in society once again, figure out how I am going to support myself financially and sustain my life, and explore employment opportunities for women who have been incarcerated, explore self-employment opportunities, set realistic goals for myself, and strive to be the best person that I can possibly be.

I hope to continue to serve my God and pray that he would bestow blessings upon me that would allow me to continue to love my neighbors, care for the less fortunate in society, be a friend to those in need, and to persevere in all the good deeds that I had done prior to being incarcerated.

If I were freed today, I would thank the judge for being merciful and for giving me a new beginning, and I would say to him "I will not disappoint you. Thank you."

And, one from her father:

I offer this letter as a character reference for Melinda, who is presently incarcerated awaiting sentencing for a violation of probation for which she did nothing more than to breathe and be alive.

There were some people in this world who were theatrically great liars and were found to be believable. Melinda is not one of those people. I know her to be honest and truthful. She spent many years in service to her family and her friends, her community, and those less fortunate in life. She would give her last dollar to someone who would come up to her and ask for money for something to eat. She would set out every earth day with yard tools, a rake, a shovel, and trash bags in hand and would go into some of the dirtiest communities and work her heart out raking and picking up trash to make the community a little cleaner and maybe a little safer for the inhabitants. She spent many nights awake as she sat up wiping the sweaty brow and cleaning up vomit of her eighteen-month-old nephew, who always got deathly ill from the chemo after being diagnosed with cancer at that tender young age. She remained loyal and dedicated to him throughout his illness. She endured months and months of intensive training to raise money and run a marathon in California in order to find a cure for cancer in children.

The newborn kitten whose mother abandoned him was fortunate to find an ally in Melinda. She came home from work every couple of hours to nurse him and care for him. She did without for herself so that she could buy birthday cards and Christmas cards and token gifts for the children of the state that she worked with so they would know that there was someone who cared. And the new leather jacket that was so desirable to Melinda? I never saw her wear it, but I did see some of her friends walking down the street in it because she knew it would make them happy. And just recently, when her eighty-nine-year-old grandmother passed away, Melinda was the one lying in the hospital bed with her, stroking her hair and telling her she loved her and that it was all right for her to leave because she will remain forever in her heart. The more I sit here and think about the years that have gone by, I keep thinking of another time and another time and another time, and the list could go on forever.

I see a history here, a history of a loving, caring, genuine, truthful person, who is paying a price far too high for all the good she had done in her life. Prison does not help in making you a better person. Prison teaches you to behave like a criminal!

Melinda is not my biological child, but I am proud for Melinda to call me "Dad," and I am happy for the opportunity to tell you that I will love and support Melinda until I take my last breath.

The judge agreed with the assessment that she was doing well and encouraged her to continue along this course of action, and he said he would review the matter in thirty days. We just kept chipping away at the evil, and the next day we would be in family court for the custody hearing.

Family court was an all-day adventure. The judge did not want the responsibility of making a decision about custody and ordered mediation. Stefan and Melinda headed off to the mediation room with the mediator, and Erin marched right in there with them. The mediator immediately asked her to leave. Stefan was uncooperative as usual, and Melinda wanted what was in the best interest of the child—joint custody. Joint custody was granted, but Erin would not allow the child to spend that weekend with his mother. She said she had to prepare the child and get him ready and used to the idea of seeing his mother. She thought she was some kind of psychiatrist—she was a secretary and an uneducated one at that.

Melinda was granted a visit with her child from two p.m. to seven p.m. However, when we arrived at daycare after we left the courthouse, Stefan had already called the daycare mother to warn her not to give us the child until five p.m. The daycare mother informed him that the court order stated two p.m. and she would follow the court order.

Bryce was so happy to see his mother. Melinda scooped him in her arms, and they hugged and hugged, and when he picked up his head from her chest, he said, "My daddy's not coming?"

And when we told him that he was not, he squealed with joy, and we had a group hug from which he lifted his head on at least three more occasions and repeated that phrase each time.

When Melinda tried to put him down he screamed, "No, Mommy!" And she had to explain that we have to put on our

Louise Baron-Kent

coats and go home. The happiness that was on his face was overwhelming, and all I could do was cry, and I was happy for him.

When we came home, he ran right over to my door, and I asked him, "Aren't you going to your house?"

He searched for recognition of his surroundings and said, "Oh yeah, my mommy's house. Yeah!" And he ran over and up the stairs in a heartbeat.

I stayed with them for a few minutes and watched him get acclimated to his stuff. He was so happy that he did not notice that I had slipped out the door so that he could reconnect with his mommy. When it was time for him to leave, he came over and kissed me and said, "See you on Monday."

When Michael came home from work that day, all we could talk about was the miracle that happened that day in court. Michael asked if he could come to chapel with me tomorrow and give thanks.

We celebrated Thanksgiving so many times that year. Our friends prepared feasts of immense proportion in our honor and in support of all the terror and loathing that we had managed to survive thus far. And the final celebration with family was heartwarming. We could now visit with our grandson and we had much to give thanks for.

Many hearings had been scheduled for Melinda's appeal, and each one ended in a continuance to another date. We were unfamiliar with the process of an appeal and had our hopes dashed after each and every hearing. The attorney general wanted Melinda to take a plea, and we insisted that she would not be taking any plea for something she did not do. But they persisted, and it was to the point of being annoying.

Melinda's status hearing was held just before Christmas. The judge was in a cranky mood, and his mood brought mine down very low indeed, and I expected the worse. Jack presented all the updated letters of character to the judge, and the attorney general hopped to attention, and I thought he would have much to say, but he said nothing. The probation representative gave a glowing report, and the judge was pleased. He said, "The probation officer is now in charge and will do any further follow-up." That was the best Christmas present ever for us. Several days later, the judge dropped dead. He would now come before the judge of all judges.

Christmas was all about family. It was truly the warmth of hearth and home and the warmth of family and friends that made life worth living. There was no need for anything further. We couldn't buy this feeling. We cherished its meaning. Our grandson and his sweetness were truly the best Christmas present ever. The New Year rekindled our spirits, and the New Year held promise and hope for rebuilding needlessly broken lives.

The things that Olga told us during our December meeting were never far from our minds. We lived in constant fear. Was she telling the truth, or was it made up? We had no way of knowing, and we needed to be ever so vigilant and let life unfold in order to find out just how much of it was true.

We did not have to wait very long before Stefan filed a restraining order against Michael. In his complaint, he mentioned how all of the neighbors were going to come in and testify for him. They were going to tell the courts how awful we were and that everyone in the neighborhood was afraid of us. These neighbors, who were so afraid of us, turned out not to be neighbors at all. They were people from the local tavern in our town who knew Michael. On the day of the hearing, it had to be postponed because none of his witnesses showed up.

Louise Baron-Kent

On the weekend, Melinda took her little one to see the *Bob the Builder* show. He loved *Bob the Builder,* and he got all decked out in his *Bob the Builder* shirt, and he had temporary tattoos on his arms. Sheer joy and excitement was an understatement of this child's exhilaration. Michael and I dropped them off at the event so they did not have to pay for parking, and we pre-arranged pickup so that it would be convenient for Melinda. I met them as they were coming out of the show, and we all walked down the street to where Michael was waiting with the vehicle. As we were walking toward the vehicle, Melinda said to me, "Oh, look. There's the prosecutor walking right in front of us. Isn't this my luck?"

The prosecutor spun around and warned Melinda, "You better be careful and remember that you are still on probation." He made his announcement on the crowded sidewalk in front of the general public. I think he acted inappropriately and unbecoming for someone with such a prestigious position, and I wondered why an assistant attorney general would have such an intense hatred of someone he had prosecuted.

Life was considerably more difficult for us now that it was snow-ing heavily, and the snow blower was no longer working. We had to shovel by hand, as we could not afford a new one because we were destitute. All of our money and resources had gone to Stefan in one form or another, whether it was paying for lawyers to defend ourselves, defending our daughter from vicious lies and false allegations, or taking care of his child. When Michael had finished shoveling, we both showered and spent the afternoon in bed relaxing and enjoying each other's company. That was the way it should be, but that was not the norm.

Our attorney subpoenaed Olga and Angelica, Stefan's former tenant, to testify in the restraining order hearing. I saw Angelica sitting behind us, and I turned and started talking to her—not about the hearing, but about her daughter. I said, "I hope your daughter is doing better."

She advised me, "She needs a kidney transplant and is on a donor list."

I assured her, "She is in my prayers every day, and I will continue to pray for her until she is whole again."

She thanked me and said, "I have no ill feelings toward you."

I assured her, "We harbor none against you or your family." All that we expected from her was for her to tell the truth. I knew what her situation was, and I did not want Stefan's evil to put her in a position to compromise herself.

When Stefan walked in and saw us talking, he came right over to them and started yelling at them, "I forbid you to speak to them."

Angelica's daughter yelled right back at him and told him, "Get away from us, and go and be with your people. Leave us alone." They clearly did not want anything to do with him. The only thing accomplished today was that a mutual temporary restraining order was issued and the hearing thereon continued to a date in the future.

Olga's information proved to be correct and forthcoming. It was unfathomable that people could deliberately hurt other people. It did not bother them one iota to tell a lie for someone. They did not mean anything to some people—they were just words. That evil was slowly killing us a little more each day. We constantly wondered when it would all end. Couldn't anyone see that there was something wrong with that man? Each night, for me, was a whole new experience in terror. When I was able to get out of bed in the morning, I was not as productive as I used to be, and I spent every waking hour afraid. Afraid of what Stefan might do to us. Afraid of what Stefan was doing to the child when he was with him. I was afraid for what he had done and might do to Melinda. I prayed to God that this nightmare would all end soon.

Sometimes when I was so worried about Melinda because her psyche was at such a very fragile point with all that she had been through in the last several years, I wanted more than ever to feel close to her and her son. In the middle of the night, I would creep into the little boy's room, and as I rested upon his bed, I was emotionally connected with him. It helped me to fall asleep and it renewed my soul until the next day.

It was Valentine's Day, our grandchild's third birthday. Michael was not out of bed yet, and this was very unusual for him. When he did arise and attempt to shower and brush his teeth, he recognized something was wrong. He looked in the bathroom mirror and did not recognize his face, and he attempted to yell, "Hon, help me. Please come upstairs."

Something was wrong. I thought I heard him say, "Please come." After rushing up the stairs and taking one look, I immediately knew that he was having a stroke. I raced down the stairs to call 911. I called Melinda, and she came right over. They arrived within minutes, did a quick assessment with symptoms that were so obvious, and helped him to walk out to the rescue truck as he had requested. They were outside for no longer than five minutes to start an IV of clot-busting drugs, informed me as to what hospital they were taking him, and they were gone in a flash.

By the time Melinda and I arrived at the hospital, Michael had already been assessed by the doctors, the CAT scans had been done and found there was no bleeding in the brain, which was a very good sign, and the effects of the two strokes he suffered had been reversed. We visited with him for four hours, but he insisted that we go about our business—he was safe now. There was nothing we needed to do or could do for him. There was too much stress in our lives. I had such a headache from this ordeal that I came home and took some aspirins and plopped myself down on the bed for a minute. Four hours later, I awoke and was uncomfortable about being alone, and it made me think about what life would be like without my husband by my side. It was a thought that I did not want to think about.

We had been in one court or another just about four out of every five days every week for the last several years. We met with numerous attorneys on numerous occasions to plan strategy and other things that it was no wonder that the official date of Melinda's final divorce almost escaped me. It was a time for renewal for everyone. Or at least that was our hope.

Surprise never ceased to amaze us. Olga, in her meeting with us in December, wanted forgiveness and understanding, but by March she had a change of heart and requested a criminal restraining order be issued against Melinda and her bail to be revoked.

We had a new custody hearing coming up shortly in April. We believed that this was part of a new plan for Olga to get this restraining order, file a motion to adjudge in contempt for some fabricated reason, and with bail revoked, Melinda would be returned to prison until the appeal could be heard. It smacked of a setup to me. Jack said that he was inclined to let them get the restraining order and that it was no big deal.

On the morning of the hearing, I sent Jack an e-mail telling him that Melinda was deathly afraid of this restraining order taking effect. We both felt that it was a setup in order to take control of a custody hearing, and that between today and the day of the custody hearing, Olga would fabricate a story that would re-incarcerate Melinda. The operative theory being that Melinda was on probation. That would be a slam-dunk for Olga. She had done this so many times before. I reminded him of all the e-mails that I had previously sent to him regarding things Olga had done to Melinda.

Jack Goodwinson met us at the entrance to the courthouse as we arrived. He told me, "I responded to your e-mail, but you had already left the house and did not get it." He told us, "You are absolutely right in your thinking and he was going to object."

Jack advised Melinda, "Do not look at the prosecutor, and no matter what she says, don't show any response. Do not shake your head to respond to the prosecutor in any fashion. Let me do my job and trust me."

The prosecutor's pitch to the judge was very negative, and Jack just stood there and smiled. I was thinking to myself that this was an awfully big trust, and I only hoped he knew what he was doing.

As I settled into my seat in the court room and looked around in disbelief as to the number of people who would be heard on that day. Uneasiness overcame me as I watched the assistant attorney general. She was a female who appeared cocky and overly confident as she glanced at Jack from time to time. I sat there straight-faced and unresponsive, and I thought to myself, *Why is Jack just standing there and smiling? Does he know something that I don't?*

The tension that I felt could be cut with a knife. As others were processed and the courtroom emptied of people, it was now the prosecutors turn to tell the judge just what an awful person Melinda was and how afraid the plaintiff was of her that she was seeking a criminal restraining order to protect the complainant until the trial date.

The judge looked directly at her and he smiled politely as he said, "Thank you." The judge turned and abruptly asked, "Mr. Goodwinson, I'd like to hear from you on this matter." The smile was suddenly replaced by a look of authority and wisdom on Jack's face as he laid everything out for the judge in an honest and concise manner, and he wasted no time in mincing words. I was in awe. We had been dealing with numerous lawyers for the last several years, but no one was like this attorney. Wow!

When Jack finished speaking, the smile was still gone from his face, and the judge looked at all of us and pronounced his ruling. The judge wasted no time in saying to the prosecutor, "I am denying your motion for the implementation of a criminal restraining order and the revocation of bail." He continued on in his ruling that he despised anyone who would use the criminal courts for their own personal edification. He further stated, "Things have been unfair enough for this young mother, and I want to assure that she will have a level playing field when it comes time for the family court matter."

It was a real victory for us, and it felt really good. When we got out into in the hall, we hugged Jack, and he hugged us back. We could not thank him enough. It was at that moment that I knew that Jack was our knight in shining armor.

We received notice that a trial on the appeal would be held some time in May and that we should be ready at a moment's notice. We met with Jack frequently, and we planned different strategies and scenarios. Jack was of the mind that he did not want to introduce much in the way of evidence and felt he could impeach the witnesses just by questioning them. He knew instinctively that anything introduced as evidence opened the door for the states' prosecutor to discredit Melinda, and he did not think that would be the right approach to drag her through the mud and cause dishonor to her. "I am not sure if I will let you testify, we will have to play this one by ear. I believe your severe depression and your PTSD would make you very vulnerable under cross-examination. You are under enough stress and don't need the prosecutor badgering you any further. I will only put you on the stand if I deemed it absolutely necessary."

He was ever mindful of Melinda's integrity. He asked me, "So what do you think?"

And I, of course, told him, "I have the utmost confidence in you." What I had seen him do thus far left me in awe, and I trusted his judgment implicitly.

We planned, and we strategized, and we reviewed. We put everyone that could in any way possible to be called as a witness on notice, and we sat and waited. The tension was unnerving, and anxiety ran high.

In August, we were still waiting to go to trial. At every pretrial conference, the state offered Melinda the plea deal, and it had always been turned down. We believed that to be a big game. We had come to recognize that no one was interested in truth. It was all about making a deal and getting someone to admit to something that they had not done.

The high point of our lives was that it was summer, and Bryce had been enjoying swimming in the pool together with some young neighbors. Although the weather had been rainy all summer, Bryce and his young friends brought joy to our lives, and we relished in the activities of the pool.

As summer was waning and the year winding down, we were hopeful that Olga's warning of Erin planning an event that would put Melinda back in prison would not come to fruition. She would complete her probation in December, and we were on the countdown. Once her probation was over, they would not have control over her life any longer. In looking ahead, we were so close. What could possibly happen at this point?

The Nightmare

2009

As summer came to an abrupt close in late August, and we prepared for the cold and drabness of fall and winter, we kept ever so close to our hearts the sunshine that would appear at the beginning of December. Family freedom would be the prize for having been joined at the hip with Melinda for the last year. That feeling was palpable and well within our reach shortly. It was so close we could taste it. It was a feeling that was beyond belief. We had no doubt that the viability of our plan would soon be realized.

During the last days of August, the neighbors started calling and asking us what was going on. We didn't even have a hint of what they could possibly be talking about. They explained that for the last several weeks the police had been watching our property and seemed to be in constant search of something or someone. We were confident that it had nothing to do with us and told the neighbors so. But when neighbors and friends continued to call, we became very afraid.

One evening, while we were enjoying the company of our grandson, the police came to Melinda's door. Melinda became so traumatized by this occurrence that she could not open her door. Instead, she called me immediately and told me what happened. As I was on the telephone with her, I could see out of my living room window that the police were still outside my property and watching.

I dropped the telephone, saying I would call her right back, and went flying out my door and into the street. I approached the officer and said, "I know you were just at my daughter's house, and I want to know if I can help you with anything?"

The young officer said, "I am here to place Melinda under arrest." He was reluctant to share any of the details of the arrest but did say that it was for an incident that happened several weeks ago.

I advised him, "If there was an incident several weeks ago and you are just now coming to speak with her, it would have to wait one more day. She is in her apartment. You frightened the hell out of her, and she has her young child with her. So unless you were about to arrest her for killing someone, it could wait for one more day."

I told the officer, "Melinda will come to the police station of her own volition the very next day to turn herself in once her child is taken to daycare and free from police intervention in this young child's life once more."

He said, "That will be acceptable." The police were not the warmest or kindest of people in this world, especially in our town. They thought nothing of slapping those cuffs on an individual right in front of their child. The police had been very good at perpetuating their actions by having the child ripped away from both mother and loving grandparents at a whim.

When I returned Melinda's telephone call, she came over to my house, and we tried to sort things out. Melinda called the police department and explained the situation, and they informed her that she was being arrested for violating a restraining order from Allen, her brother-in-law. They alleged that on Friday evening, August 14, Melinda violated a restraining order by driving by his house.

She said to them, "This is impossible, as I have been out of town and can prove it. Allen doesn't have a restraining order against me." The water main on the main thoroughfare had burst and the water department closed the main street to traffic. Allen lived on the very next street, which was the detour road for the street closure. So he may have seen her vehicle, but it was not she who was driving it.

However, the police would hear none of it and informed her, "You can tell it to the judge."

As we sat there discussing the situation and trying to absorb the absurdity of these allegations, we had a flashback to our meeting with Olga. She had told us that Stefan's mother was planning something for taking care of Melinda once again. It became quite transparent, and we could clearly see that this was Erin keeping her promise. She could not get Olga to help her out anymore; Stefan was a lousy witness and of no help; Kathy wanted nothing to do with that anymore and wanted her life to get back to normal; Erin personally was responsible for having Melinda terminated from her employment; Jim was the star witness in the conviction and the upcoming appeal; Allen was the only one left that she could have control over. Allen was her next recruit.

My next telephone call was to Jack Goodwinson. I explained the situation to him, and I told him what my plan of action was, and he asked that I give him a call back and give him all the particulars on arraignment and charges, etc. After I finished discussing the situation with Jack, I then called Melinda's family court attorney, who was in shock that they were still at it and, once again, just before a family court hearing. I also explained the course of action that we had planned and that I was working with Jack on that matter. He also asked me to call him the next day to tell him of the outcome.

True to my word, Melinda and I went to the police station after four p.m. If there was anything that we had learned through the last several years of dealing with the police, it was to get arraigned after a certain hour. All of the rookies work the second shift, and the courts were closed so they could not transport a prisoner to the courthouse to be arraigned by the judge. They called in a justice of the peace, and, if appropriate, they'd release her on bail. It was an oversight on account of inexperience when they released Melinda on bail. She tried to be honest with them and told them she was on probation. However, they could not find any record of that. She was subsequently released on bail and given an arraignment date.

When I called Jack to give him the information, he told me that the date was not convenient for him. I became frightened, and Jack told me to relax, that he would handle everything. From my previous experience with dealing with him, I felt confident and secure in his abilities. He told us to ignore the date that was given to us, relax, and enjoy the holiday weekend. She would be arraigned after the weekend, and he would keep us apprised as to the date.

Louise Baron-Kent

When the assigned arraignment date arrived, Stefan spent the entire day at his house, which was three houses away from ours, and was outside gyrating and jubilating in his usual fashion and scoping out our house. When the day passed and no arraignment took place, Stefan became infuriated. He had already made plans for that weekend to spend time with his parents and his child and girlfriend out of state. He planned on Melinda being incarcerated; perhaps even a little extended vacation would be in order for him. But his plan went south, as it was Melinda's weekend with the child, and he had no choice but to relinquish the child to her. Erin's plan, thus far, had no impact.

I was quite sure he called his attorney, Skip Baldini, but even he would not be foolish enough to tangle with Jack Goodwinson. Jack was politically on the right side of the fence and was the former attorney general and held a lot of power. Babs Baldini, an assistant attorney general, long standing, had her eye on one of the vacant judgeships. Political suicide could be at hand for any interference from the Baldinis. Would that be a risk they were willing to take?

Jack called on the day after the holiday and informed us of the date for the arraignment. It was scheduled for the following day, and he instructed us to present before the "hanging judge," as I had always called him. Jack knew he truly was but could not use that term. He told us to bring plenty of cash for the bail.

Because I had spent my entire career working in the law with various law firms and had been trained well to do my legwork and prepare, prepare, prepare, prior to going in front of the judge, that was exactly what I did. I was not aware of any order of Allen. I knew that the previous July, Kathy had her restraining order renewed while Melinda was incarcerated. But I could not recall Allen having one.

I set off to check the records of the clerk where criminal family court restraining orders were recorded. While I was questioning one of the clerks about an order, the rotund black clerk recognized me and came over to say, "Hello, how are things going?"

I told her my tale of woe, and she pulled Melinda's file. She informed me, "There is no restraining order for Allen, and the one for Kathy was not valid because it was *never* served on Melinda."

I asked, "Are you sure?"

She explained, "the white copy of this attached two-page set is the original and the green copy was the copy to be served on the defendant." She stated, "Furthermore, the acknowledgement for service, complete with the date that it was served, was blank and, therefore, not served and was not in place." She then proceeded to hand me both copies—the white and the green—and said, "Now she was served as of this date!" I thanked her and placed the copies in my tote bag.

Anne, the friend and advocate of Melinda, was notified as common courtesy of what would be happening and what our plan of action was in case she wanted to be present in the courtroom for the arraignment.

On Wednesday, September 2, 2009, the arraignment day for Melinda, we presented before the hanging judge who did the arraignments on the district court level. He was just as mean and belligerent as he had always been on previous occasions when Melinda had been arraigned. He barked and made every attempt to intimidate us. My saving grace was that Jack was here with us. The judge barked for me to post two thousand dollars in bail before a certain time, and I smiled and thanked him; I was overly prepared for this drunkard. I was not shaking in my shoes or crying this time. I was meeting it head on. Jack made every effort to get the charges dropped, citing the lack of jurisdiction of the police department to press charges when, in fact, there was no restraining order.

The judge attempted to cut him down to size and ordered Melinda cuffed and sent to the holding cell for a free ride to the prison. I was shocked at the power that this alcohol-addicted judge had over someone's life. I was determined not to pay the bail if they were taking her to prison anyway. The rules for this arrest were very different from any other of Melinda's arrests because this was originally a district court case where she was found guilty and on probation. But it also was on appeal to the superior court, and so the punishment and consequences just kept compounding. This infuriated Jack. The judge barked his word as final and referred us to the superior court for the double whammy.

In courtroom 12M, the superior court forum, the assistant attorney general was a little upset that earlier that morning the town prosecutor did not cite Melinda as a probation violator. The attorney general insisted that there would be no bail and that Melinda would be imprisoned. After much going round and round between the judge, the assistant attorney general, and Jack Goodwinson, they agreed to a date for a violation of probation hearing of September 16, 2009.

The sheriff went up to Melinda and said something in her ear and she began to cry. Jack said to the judge, "For God's sake, how many times are you going to punish this woman for the same crime?" Jack then left the courtroom in a hurry.

I mouthed to Anne that I would meet her at my car in a few minutes. I believed it was over, and I believed she also thought it was over.

What I did not know was that the assistant attorney general referred Melinda back to Judge Hobbitt to be presented as a probation violator and to be incarcerated until the September 16 hearing date.

As I was following Jack down to the third floor, he began using expletives and stomping his feet and slamming the doors. I said to Jack, "You just keep going where you have to go and I will stay right behind you and catch up with you."

He said as he hustled down the hall way at a fast pace, "If they put Melinda in prison today, I am going to the Supreme Court tomorrow and filing a petition there, and she will definitely be freed. That was clearly an abuse of power."

When we got before Judge Hobbitt again, the judge said, "I will not hear it. If your client is going to prison, it is just too bad. You need to take this up with the attorney general."

Jack explained, "We just had a hearing in Superior Court and have a date scheduled for a violation and/or bail hearing."

The judge closed him out and said, "My decision is final." The judge quickly left the bench so that he did not have to deal with Jack any longer.

Once again, Jack stormed out of the courtroom with more expletives and steam coming out of his ears, and I ran along right behind him, as I did not know what was going on. We went back up to 12M, and he went up to the assistant attorney general and explained the situation and told him he needed him down before Hobbitt for a hearing before the judge. He agreed to come to the courtroom once he finished with the remaining prisoners before Judge Grillo. Once again, we left courtroom 12M and raced down to courtroom 3D and waited.

The attorney general eventually came down, and he refused to let Melinda go free, even though Jack firmly told him there was no probable cause on which to hold her. The restraining order was in the name of Kathy, and Allen brought the complaint, and, furthermore, the restraining order was never served on Melinda and, therefore, was invalid. The assistant attorney general would not budge. As I was sitting there—and by now quite obviously shaking in my boots—waiting to see what would happen next, Jack said to the attorney general, "Where are your balls? Be a man. Make the decision. You have the authority to make this decision!"

The assistant attorney general, with his head hung very low, said to Jack, "I am not in a position to make that decision."

That statement clearly led me to believe that someone at the attorney general's office (Babs Baldini?) told him to persist at all costs—right, wrong, or indifferent! The female clerk sitting in front of the empty judges' mount asked Jack, "What is your final decision?"

He said, "I don't know. It is up to the assistant attorney general, and he is not budging."

She told him, "The judge will not hear you. The judge left me in charge to note your final decision in the record—end of story."

At that point, Jack slammed his papers and file down on the desk in front of the clerk and began pounding with his index finger and said to her, "I want to be heard. You get that judge out here. I demand to be heard!" He was very forceful and scared everyone in the courtroom. She got up and went out of the room.

In the meantime, while we were waiting for her return, a heavyset sheriff came over to me as I sat crying and shaking in my seat and said, "I know that you are Melinda's mother. I know because I have seen you in Judge Hobbitt's courtroom many times before. You have a wonderful daughter. I know her. You should not worry. Everything will turn out for the best." That was of very little comfort to me because I knew that there was not a thing that he could do to help me.

After he and I spoke about Melinda's psychopathic husband for a few minutes, he left, and another older sheriff with glasses came right into the aisle where I was seated. He came up to me and said, "I am so sorry for all that you are going through, but I want you to know that Jack has been here all day fighting for Melinda. Whatever you paid that attorney, he was worth every penny, because he's on your side. I never saw an attorney who believed so strongly in his client in a criminal matter." We had been treated so shabbily by the judicial system that the outpouring of kindness and consideration of many of the sheriffs in the courtroom that day overwhelmed me.

A few minutes later, Judge Hobbitt came to the bench, red faced, and began barking, "She is going to prison, and that is that!"

Jack told the judge, "You will hear me, because if you do not, you are abusing your power and encouraging and allowing the attorney general to perpetuate a malicious prosecution case." Jack went on to tell the judge, "Kathy did, at one point in time, have a restraining order against Melinda. However, it was not she who filed the complaint."

The judge said, "It doesn't matter if Melinda were out on the street in front of Kathy's house, regardless of whether or not she was even home, then Melinda was in violation of the restraining order." Then Jack brought up the fact that no restraining order was presently in existence because it was never served on Melinda, and, therefore, if there was no knowledge, then there was no order.

The judge said, "I will incarcerate Melinda until the next day, and that will give us time to check the court records to see if the order had been served or not."

Jack said, "This will not be necessary because Melinda's mother had gone to the clerk's office and picked up the original that was never served from the magistrate's clerk, and she has it with her."

Hobbitt looked me squarely in the eye and asked, "Do you in fact have it?"

I said, "Yes, I certainly do." I put on my glasses and rummaged through my tote bag and pulled out the original and handed it to the sheriff, which he, in turn, handed to the judge.

Hobbitt rumbled on about how it was not possible that the order was not served on Melinda, and then he kept reading down farther. For the first time that day—as a matter of fact, for the first time ever since I had been dealing with him—I saw him acting human. That to me was a very scary happening. His eyes got big as saucers, and he announced in a quiet and mellow voice, "This case cannot go forward."

He looked at the assistant attorney general and told him, "You must dismiss this case, and if you won't, I am going to dismiss it." He said to Jack, "There is no valid restraining order in existence, and Allen does not have a restraining order against Melinda."

He looked at me and said, in a very humane and kind voice, "I know that you have paid bail money, and I want you to go right down there now and get your money back." Little did he know that I had no intention of paying the courts thousands of dollars for him to imprison my daughter. He had no way of knowing that I had not complied with his order.

Jack informed the judge, "Stefan and his family personally use the police department and the courts for their own edification to have Melinda arrested every time there is an issue of custody before the family court."

Hobbitt called Jack to the bench and told him exactly what to say in the dismissal stipulation and said, "Do it now." The entire drama played out in less than an hour, but the intensity of the situation made that time seem like an eternity. Had I not gone to the courthouse and gotten that original restraining order from the clerk of the magistrate, we would have gotten quite a different result on that day.

Melinda was finally released, and when we walked out of the courtroom, Melinda and I embraced and cried together. The sheriff with the glasses came over to me again and said, "I never speak to any of the family members or have much interaction with the prisoners, but I feel there is something about you and the way Jack was fighting so hard for you that I feel compelled to come over to you once again." He wished us luck.

Jack, Melinda, and I all met in the hallway, and we all hugged and then went our separate ways with Jack telling me, "We will talk in a few days."

As we parted, Jack started running back down the hall toward us and said, "The judge finally got it—he really got it," and Jack was pleased. He also said, "I am on my way to meet with the chief of the criminal division of the attorney general's office. I have words of wisdom that I want to share about some of the workers in the attorney general's office." Later that evening, Jack sent me an e-mail telling me that he had a very long and productive meeting with the chief. Knowing Jack, I was sure he did not just scratch the surface, I was sure that he went through the whole Melinda portmanteau.

It was a hard-fought battle, but the victory was ever so sweet. If anyone could have gotten a case dismissed at arraignment, it was Jack Goodwinson. He was a real powerhouse. Being involved in all of Melinda's criminal cases and seeing the ineptness and abuse that prevailed just drained a person of every ounce of strength that it took to endure. When it was over and I was home, I did not function. It was a period of three to four days for everything to decompress before I could get on with life once again.

Melinda called the daycare on our way home to tell them that she would be there shortly to pick up her child, but she was told that Stefan had already picked up the child, and he told them that Melinda was in prison. She called her family court attorney, and he called Stefan's attorney, Skip Baldini, and Baldini ordered him to relinquish that child forthwith to its mother. We met Stefan at the police station and picked up little Bryce. Erin also showed up in a separate vehicle, and they were both madder than wet hens. We believed they were both there at the police station so that they could question the police as to why Melinda was not in prison.

My grandson was never so happy to see his mother. He told us his father told him that his mother left him and went away on a vacation. Although on previous occasions, he came right out and told the child that his mother was going back to prison. The director of the daycare heard him tell that to his child. Thursday, after Melinda brought Bryce to daycare, the director of the daycare called Melinda aside and told her that she heard Stefan saying mean and nasty things to the child and said that if there was a possibility of testifying in court, she would be happy to do so, as she believed that Stefan was an unfit parent.

By the time I was finally able to follow up with Melinda's advocate, Anne, it was the next day, and she was quite anxious to know the outcome. She believed she had experienced the outcome with the morning session. When I told her, "This turned out to be an all-day adventure culminating in Melinda's release and charges being dismissed," she was in shock. When she believed the hearing to be over and Melinda being cuffed and sent to prison—the point that I also believed was its ending—there was no way for me to let her know that it was not over. It was just the beginning, and I went on to elaborate exactly what had happened. I told her, "Jack has been good for us," and Anne was in complete agreement.

The Moment of Truth

We celebrated Melinda's birthday on October 31. It was a wonderful occasion; it was not only the day of her birth, but it was also the day of Halloween. It was a day of celebration for all children and a day of celebration of when this wonderful human being blessed the earth with her presence.

Nothing had been forthcoming about the superior court appeal. It had been more than a year since the appeal was filed and just one month away from her being released from all criminal sanctions that loomed large above our heads. We were led to believe that the trial would take place in May, and our lives had been on hold since that time. A moment's notice of readiness did not allow for anything but home confinement.

As we celebrated yet another year of Melinda's life, the telephone rang, and it was Jack. He asked me, "What are you doing in the next couple of days?" He brought a smile to my face.

I laughed a little and said, "The same thing that I have been doing since May—waiting for the trial."

He laughed back at me and said, "We will be in court on November 4."

I was excited for the most part but apprehensive too. I said, "Yeah, right, we've heard this all before. It was always nothing more than hurry up and wait!"

He asked, "Please come to my office on Monday so that we can prepare. This is truly it," he told us, and, "once again, the offer of a plea agreement is still available." He knew what our answer would be, but he said, "I would be remiss in my representation if I didn't offer that to you once again." It was our decision wholly, and he encouraged, "think it through from every angle so that you are sure you are making the right decision."

On Monday we met in Jack's office, and we reviewed all of the information; we reviewed the actual recording of the transcripts of Olga's meeting with us so that he could identify the exact location on the recording of where she was saying specific words like "liar" and "I lied" or "I did this for Stefan and his mother" for ease of sharing with the prosecutor in discrediting Olga and impeaching her testimony.

He told us, "I really don't want to have to use that transcript or recording in court." He was of the mind that he could impeach Olga's testimony without having to resort to evidence of the meeting. He knew that if he used it, it would open the door for the prosecutor to bring into evidence everything that we discussed on that day, and he believed that could be detrimental to Melinda's case.

He said, "I believe that Melinda has been through enough already, and she doesn't need to be dragged through the mud any further."

However, the transcript would serve as a powerful backup if things should get ugly. Jack absolutely did not want to put Melinda on the stand because of her depression and vulnerability at this time in her life. He did not stop there though; he prepared her just as if she would be put on the stand—a backup plan—just in case. No stone was left unturned with Jack, and that was what we loved about him so much. He gave us copies of the entire packet of discovery from the state's case and told us to bring them home and review them.

That would be a very interesting case, and we were prepared beyond belief. Even though we were so well prepared, we were all nervous and quite apprehensive, and we knew that sleep would not come easily on Tuesday evening.

Wednesday arrived, and we were all out of bed way before we should have been. We fortified ourselves with a hearty break-fast, and we were on our way before we knew it. We arrived at the courthouse with our heads held high and knots in the pits of our stomachs.

As we were walking down the hallway, headed to the assigned courtroom, a woman grabbed my arm and pulled me to her. I looked down, and it was Olga. Surprise overtook me as I asked her, "What is it that you want?"

She told me, "Everything is good."

"What does that mean?" I snapped.

She said, "I am not going to get on that stand to testify against Melinda."

I pulled my arm away from her grasp, and I walked away and caught up with Melinda and Michael in the courtroom.

When I got into the courtroom, there was Michael and Melinda talking to Melinda's attorney, who was with us at the time of the meeting in December and Melinda's advocate, Anne.

There was no one else in the room. I thought it the perfect opportunity to pull out my blessed and holy salt to pray and purify the room before the trial began. As I pulled out my little bottle, Melinda's attorney, who knew how I was with my religious rituals, said, "You're not!"

And I replied, "Watch me!" as I began my prayer and walked over to the jury box and commenced sprinkling. Then I walked over to the table, where both plaintiff and defendant resided during the trial and prayed and sprinkled there, and, having a small amount left over, I went to the judge's bench and performed my ritual there too. When I had finished, we all looked at each other in amazement, and we laughed.

Shortly thereafter, all parties related to this criminal trial entered the courtroom. The judge was the last to enter. The judge commenced by explaining to everyone in the courtroom what the procedures were that we would be following. He explained how the jury would be selected and how they would be questioned. His dissertation filled most of the morning, and then he called a recess.

During the recess, Jack asked me if I could get him some batteries for his tape player. His were dead, and he had not remembered to check his equipment before he left the office that morning. I was more than a little surprised by his failure to do so, as Jack was always overly prepared. Michael and I left the courtroom in search of batteries. I had a friend who worked in the building next to the courthouse, and I thought it prudent to pay her a visit rather than search for a store where we could buy some. It turned out to be a great idea. We were back at the court in a flash.

As we walked down the hallway toward the courtroom, we noticed that Olga was still sitting on a bench outside the courtroom. With the amount of people milling around outside the courtroom, we knew that the court was still in recess.

I went into the courtroom, and Jack and the prosecutor were talking about the case. I gave him the batteries in case he wanted to play the tape for the prosecutor during the recess. Melinda, Michael, and I went down to the coffee shop for a quick drink. One of the prosecutors was in line in front of us, along with five other prosecutors from the attorney general's office. We heard them talking among themselves and saying, "That woman is going down, and we are all here to help bring that woman down and send her to prison." Imagine six prosecutors. They were pretty determined. It infuriated me to know that precious resources were being wasted in our recessive economy to bring down someone who did nothing, someone whom they did not know personally, and on a misdemeanor charge. We were sure that was being done at the instruction of someone much higher up in the attorney general's office. Murderers, rapists, bank robbers, and other real criminals were being freed from prison or not tried and given very favorable deals because resources were so scarce. But that poor young mother had been doggedly pursued by, not one, but six prosecutors for a misdemeanor crime of "disorderly conduct." That was unimaginable. That pursuit had been ongoing for over a year.

The judge called all involved back to the courtroom, and jury selection began. In all of my years working in the law, I had never had reason to see, never mind take part in, a criminal trial in superior court. It was interesting, and, at the same time, it was very scary. These men and women were all strangers to us, and the fate of our daughter would be in their hands. It was a little unnerving.

Around one p.m. the judge called for the lunch recess. Seating the jury would be completed after the lunch break, and the trial would begin shortly thereafter. We all went out to a nice restaurant close to the courthouse and had a bite to eat. Jack did not join us, as he wanted to check out some things pertaining to the trial at his office. When he was representing a person, he took it very seriously, and he was always working on the situation. He did not stop until the job was complete.

When we got back from lunch, Olga was still sitting in the hallway outside of the courtroom. As we went by her, she attempted to get my attention once again. I ignored her and kept on walking with Melinda, Michael, and Melinda's other attorney. The two alternate jurors were selected, the jury was seated in a swift manner, and the trial commenced.

Jack and the prosecutor made opening statements. The prosecutor in his opening statement had nothing good to say about Melinda. He became so engrossed and energetic in his belittling and depreciating of Melinda's character that he became animated to a dangerous level as he thrust his index finger in her face and got closer and closer and louder and louder and yelled, red faced, "She is guilty of the crime and needs to be punished."

The judge stopped him and reminded him, "This is my courtroom, and I will do the chastising, if appropriate, and there is a presumption of innocence here. The jury will decide if she is guilty or not." He was so full of drama. He encouraged the prosecutor to calm himself and proceed accordingly. The whole drama played out in a somewhat more civilized manner after that.

I tried very desperately to sit there and to have no expression on my face. People from the jury looked my way from time to time, and what I saw was a softness about them. They did not smile or look at me in any particular manner that would indicate that they were siding with the defense, but rather, I just felt a sense of compassion and a connection with them.

The first witness called was Olga. In she came and perched in the witness box. The jury was void of expression as they looked at her and listened to what she had to say. When questioned by the prosecutor, she recounted, "Melinda came up to me in the family courthouse and said some awful things to me and made me feel bad."

The prosecutor asked, "Did she touch you or assault you in any manner?"

She replied, "She did not touch me." She gave an account of where she was standing when the incident happened and that she was at the family court to give testimony in her boyfriend's divorce hearing.

She was then questioned by Jack, who immediately handed her the complaint that she filed with the capitol police which stated, "Melinda walked right up to me and poked me in the chest and said mean things to me."

Jack asked, "Please clarify your testimony for the prosecution as opposed to your complaint. Which is it? Did she or did she not touch you?"

She answered by saying that the capitol police must have misunderstood what she was saying and therefore, the discrepancy. Jack proceeded with, "But you read the sworn statement. You swore the statements in your complaint were all true, and then you signed it, didn't you?"

"Yes," she said, "but I must have been mistaken. I know that she did not touch me."

"So what you are saying then, is that you lied?"

She answered, "Yes." And she hung her head as she said it.

Jack said, "I have no further questions of this witness."

Jim, who had fabricated the entire scenario with Olga, was called next to testify. He told the jury that he was "Santa Claus," and his physical appearance was that of Santa Claus. He was soft spoken as he told the jury, "I work every Christmas at the mall and pose for pictures with good little boys and girls." He had a bushy, white beard and bushy, white eyebrows, and he looked to be a kindly old man. But that was a travesty committed against the children of our town who flocked to the mall to have their pictures taken with that man every Christmas. For in reality, he may look like Santa Claus on the outside, but on the inside he was nothing more than a liar not worthy of the adoration of any child.

His testimony was similar to Olga's, but he claimed, "We were standing in a particular location," which was different from the location that Olga testified to, and he stated, "Melinda came up to Olga and physically assaulted her and said nasty things to her, causing her to become upset and afraid for her life."

When Jack questioned Jim, he had him draw out how they were standing in the hallway of the court on a piece of paper, the same as he had done with Olga. He thanked Jim and told him, "I have no more questions for you."

The judge announced, "The hour is late, and this forces us to adjourn for today. You are to return tomorrow for the continuation of the trial." He excused the jury and cautioned, "Do not talk or discuss among yourselves anything you have heard here today." We all rose to allow the jury and the judge to exit the courtroom. It was over for the day.

As we were standing and gathering our belongings, the clerk of the court came over to us and said, "This is none of my business, but what the heck did your husband ever see in that thing?"

We all looked at each other, and we laughed at her naivety and shrugged our shoulders that we did not know.

We met up with Jack on the way out, and we talked as we walked. He asked, "Are you all comfortable with what happened in the courtroom?"

We all said in unison, "We're all comfortable, and whatever strategy you employ, we have the utmost faith in your abilities, and we defer to your expertise." He smiled and shook our hands, and we made plans to meet back at the courthouse the next morning.

When we arrived home, we did anything and everything to keep busy and kept our minds off the trial. But, as hard as we tried, it always popped into our consciousness. There would be minimal sleeping that night also.

The next morning we were back at the courthouse, and neither Olga nor Jim was there. We arrived early enough so that I could go "a salting," and no one looked surprised at my actions. Before long Melinda's family court lawyer showed up, and he would be the last witness for the case and the one and only witness for the defense.

Of course, there was the whole procedural thing that took place, and that took about forty-five minutes to an hour. The judge made his statement, the jury was reseated, and then the judge made another dissertation for the benefit of the jurors. Before long the witness was called.

Melinda's family court attorney testified, "I was present in the courthouse all of that day representing Melinda. At the time the incident allegedly occurred, everyone was on a break and in the hallway. I could see Melinda at all times, and no incident or commotion occurred." He gave witness as to where each of the two complaining witnesses were standing in the hallway at the time of the incident, and it was inconsistent with the other two inconsistencies of the two previous witnesses, Jim, witness in support of complainant, and Olga, the complainant.

The prosecutor, in his cross-examining, alluded to the fact that because Melinda was his client he would come on the stand and lie for her. The attorney was livid at that attack on his character and made it quite clear in his answer, "I am an officer of the court. I've been practicing law for a long period of time, and I have never compromised my integrity in any way for any client."

The judge was a little shocked at the attack on a brother attorney. He commented as to the inappropriateness of such an attack and called a recess. Once the jury had filed past the bench and was out of earshot of the judge, he continued to chastise the young attorney for the manner in which he treated other members of the bar, which was also a direct attack on the judicial system as a whole in his estimation. He continued on with his disquisition as everyone left the room and welcomed a break.

Our whole entourage left the area and assembled out in the courtyard for a breath of fresh air, away from the accusations of the prosecutor whose actions were more that of a bully than a professional person doing a professional job. It was easily detected that his hatred was personal. Something was driving this man to win at all costs. He was really pushing for the jury to believe the testimony of the two sociopathic complainants over the testimony of an officer of the court, a brother attorney, and an honorable man. But we left that all behind in the courtroom and were now enjoying small talk and ideas unrelated to the trial at hand. It was a welcome breath of fresh air being outside with such caring individuals. We were in the presence of people who knew us and understood what was really going on here. The only thing that we knew for sure here was that the ride would soon be over, and it would be time to get off. But where we would get off was the unknown.

Reality quickly set in, as it was time to head back to the courtroom. When we arrived in the courtroom, Jack, who remained behind to pull together his closing argument, pulled me aside and asked, "Are you comfortable with the case that was presented?"

I, once again, told him, "I'm pleased with everything you've done." I did not think of him as bold or aggressive, but as honest and caring about each and every individual that testified before that jury. Jack then informed me, "I'm not going to call any further witnesses, nor will I present any further evidence. The defense will rest."

Once again, I told him, "If you're comfortable with what you presented to the jury, then I defer to your judgment. You're the expert, and you know when enough is enough."

Jack sat down at the defense table, and Melinda joined him. The prosecutor was already in place at the prosecution table, and it was time to recall the jury. The judge asked both sides if there were any further witnesses. Each replied in the negative and rested their case.

Jack, in his closing argument, painted a picture of Melinda, whose goals in life were to be productive and take care of her child. He filled the jury with a brief snippet as he told them, "Melinda was an abused and battered wife, and her spouse is an evil person who felt compelled to diminish the quality of life of his former wife to zero. He has accomplished this through the complicity of his family and girlfriends."

The prosecutor in his closing argument agreed with Jack as he told the jury, "The man behind this whole ordeal is a bad person—one who lied and cheated and used people, but I implore you to find Melinda guilty of the crime of disorderly conduct and punish her accordingly."

The judge now took over control of the proceedings. He explained the charges against the defendant, and he explained each and every element of the crime alleged. He went on to instruct the jury that each and every element of the crime must be met in order to convict. If each and every element had not been accounted for, then no crime would have been committed. The judge was very lengthy and thorough in his charge to the jury. I found this judge to be fair and impartial. Upon completion of his charge to the jury, the jury stood, faces expressionless, with nary a look in the direction of the defendant as they filed out of the courtroom and into the jury deliberation room.

It was now out of our hands, and we would once again wait. We had all sorts of questions in our minds, but we would not allow ourselves the liberty of contemplating any of them. We tried to remain upbeat.

Anne, Melinda's advocate, wondered out loud when she said to me, "Why is this case so important to the attorney general? Why has he expended precious resources on such a trivial case of trying to blame a little boy's mother, who is a victim of domestic violence and who is in the process of an acrimonious divorce proceeding?"

She was somewhat disappointed that the jury wouldn't hear all of the horrible stuff that happened prior to these complaints being filed, and they would never hear anything about the persistent litigations that pulled a family court case into numerous criminal courts. They would not know that this was a planned strategy, which was now known as domestic violence by proxy. At the beginning of the trial she said, "I'm so excited, because finally all of the bad stuff will come out, and everyone will see Stefan for what he really is."

Our position was explained to Anne. She was told all of the downside of bringing all of that information to the forefront, and Jack was ever mindful of Melinda's integrity. That was first and foremost in Jack's estimation, and he did not see the need to dredge anything out of the past no matter how painful the testimony would have been or the impact it would have had on the jury. It was good information that could easily be turned against the individual by the twisting of facts, and he thought it best to let sleeping dogs lie. In her heart, she knew that was the right decision that Jack made, and she knew how much we trusted Jack.

It seemed that the jury had just retired for deliberation when we received a phone call to return to the courtroom, as the jury had reached its decision. Horror was the first emotion felt by all of us. The moment of truth had arrived.

It had only been about twenty minutes for the jury to retire to the deliberation room and make their decision. When the jury entered the courtroom, everyone at the defense and prosecution table stood in respect of the jury. As the jury paraded before the defendant, they were all smiling at her—laughing and making light of the situation. Melinda, with all that she had been through in the last couple of years, was thinking, *They're sending me to prison, and they're all laughing about it.* She was worried and could not control her emotions and began to cry uncontrollably.

The entire formal process of deciding that case took less than one hour. Their decision was made swiftly and unanimously— "Not guilty!"

Upon the jury being discharged after the rendering of their verdict, they all passed Melinda and touched her shaking, contorted body on the hand or the arm in a show of solidarity and comforting. Melinda placed her hand on each and every hand of the jurors and thanked them.

Melinda's attorney—who was with us at the time of the fateful December meeting and who thought for sure she would be one of the star witnesses in that hearing, but in actuality never got to testify—rushed off to the jury pool room to question the jurors about their verdict. As she questioned them, they told her that they did not believe anything that the two complaining witnesses said. They found them to be unbelievable, and the relationship between Stefan and his girlfriend questionable and suspect. That, coupled with the fact that the corroborating witness was Jim, made their testimony even more incredible. And, in line with what the clerk had been thinking the previous day, they said that Stefan must have been desperate for something to have a relationship with her. What the parameters of that relationship were—no one wanted to know.

It was as if a huge weight had been lifted from our shoulders. We could now breathe and perhaps begin to put our lives back in order. Our next milestone would be December 3, which would truly be a day of freedom. It would be the day when all of her criminal penalties would be over and Melinda would no longer be under the control of Stefan, his family, or anyone else.

Louise Baron-Kent

The Rebirth

It had been some time, approximately nine months, since Melinda had been last arrested. To us, it appeared that we had weathered the storm. However, it is important for us to remain ever vigilant and to not let our guards down. We go to bed every evening, and we are still afraid. We are afraid for what could happen on a whim. We are always cognizant of the fact that there was and still is no protection for us, not from the police, not from the courts, not from anyone. We hear sirens, and we immediately hop to attention in fear.

Our conditioning is very recognizable. Our lives will never be carefree as they once had been, and that fear would be forever in our hearts and would govern all of our actions for the foreseeable future and maybe the remainder of our lives. The important totality of our lives is that we held on tight to each other through the very worst of this ordeal, and we triumphantly emerged robust and stronger than ever. We are truly a much more solid family unit than we had ever thought possible after all that we had endured. Our hearts swell with excitement when we feel the warmth of the sun and know that we are still alive.

There is not a day that passes that Stefan fails to drive by our house or park in the driveway of his house and harass us, try to bully us, yell obscenities at us, or anything else he can think of that will annoy us in his usual juvenile fashion. He constantly makes trips to the police station to file some sort of complaint about something we supposedly did, regardless of whether or not we have even seen him on that day. It is usually something he has been obsessing about for the day. The police find him believable. We find that unbelievable. We find it hard to believe that all this time has passed, and he is still engaged in the behaviors of three years prior. It must serve some purpose for him because we actually can look at him now engaging in these behaviors and laugh at him in amazement that someone can be so immature.

Stefan calls Melinda almost daily, sometimes four or five times a day, to tell her what an awful mother she is or that she should be more like him—a good person and a good parent. The messages are always the same. He tells her how wonderful he is and how awful she is. Different day, same message, it amounts to nothing more than pure harassment. We have no choice but to endure. We have no idea if this ordeal is truly over or whether Stefan and his family will continue in their dogged determination to be the final genesis in Melinda's ultimate demise.

We have absolutely nothing left; we are destitute. We live each day from hand to mouth. The cost to help Melinda finalize her divorce, defend her through her numerous arrests and incarcerations, and the attempts of Stefan and friends against

Michael and I has cost us just under a half a million dollars, and we know in our hearts that we are not done yet. We are back to square one, because Stefan still has placement of our grandchild and has the final say as to what happens in that child's life. It is important to us to have this child removed from the care of this psychopathic person.

Had there not been so much corruption in our state's family court system, and had the judges done their jobs in a professional manner, and had the attorneys used "common sense" as an indicator instead of "dollars and cents" as the criteria for good representation, the outcome of who had care, custody, and control of this precious child would have been very different. The courts and the judges were not interested in looking at the cases of any court other than their own, and often did not search beyond the instant hearing to see what was actually happening in an individual's life. Melinda's child was removed from her custody because she had been imprisoned. Therefore, she was perceived as having abandoned her child. If only the judge had looked to see what really happened and why or how her imprisonments came to be, he would have seen that it was all a part of the plan of a psychopath, Stefan, to gain custody of the child and deliver the ultimate betrayal to Melinda by having her child taken from her, in addition to all of her other worldly possessions including her dignity.

Neither did the judge look back to any of the testimony obtained during the trial of the matter where he chastised Stefan on numerous occasions for having something wrong with him or of being drunk or on drugs. The judge who had been so controlling in his "political correctness," being the norm in his courtroom during his pre-retirement tenure, now in his retirement or *per diem* tenure, enters the courtroom sucking on breath mints or candy to freshen his breath. Before long his ostentatious and pompous personality gives way to joking and making light of every situation. He has personal conversations with attorneys about their clients and laughs at them.

In all of the three years that Melinda had been involved with this family court justice, I have never observed this reckless and unprofessional behavior from a judge. This judge, who actually chastised anyone who mentioned the word *God* in his courtroom, was now preaching, and on more than one occasion, "we are all children of God." I began to question myself as to whether or not I was really experiencing what I thought I was experiencing. He continued on in open court to comment on how boring the courts are on procedural wording, and that it was incumbent upon him to create new words to liven things up a little. There was no holding him back on this day, and he proceeded to comment that he was in such a good mood that perhaps someone might think that he is "on something!" That was all I needed to hear. It was shocking to my sensibilities, and I perceived his last comment as a gross understatement.

And the family court attorney, knowing that Melinda had no job and her resources were scarce, abandoned his loyalty to his client and sided with the attorney representing Stefan, who was self-employed and had sufficient funds to still demand loyalty for the money he paid for his representation.

Although the crying has stopped for the most part, Melinda has paid a very high price for loving and being married to a psychopath. She is a well-educated woman who worked in a professional capacity caring for the children of the state. She will never work in her profession for the remainder of her days. More than likely, this educated woman will never be employable by anyone because of her criminal record. Employers are very much like the rest of society. It is their job to determine if the individual has ever been arrested.

The economy, in addition to our personal lives, has been tanked and added to the impossibility of any hope of Melinda finding meaningful employment. It will be our responsibility to help reinvent Melinda's life in some fashion and develop some self-employed status in order for her to participate under the radar of a society that treats people who have been incarcerated, for whatever reason, like the dog poop on the bottom of someone's shoe. This will be no easy task, but it is our next challenge, and we will keep on until we are successful.

Stefan is no longer represented by Skip Baldini, but the tensions between the police department and our family have not diminished. Mr. Baldini has done his job well to defame the good name of our family. The police have our names carved in stone as trouble. This I fear will follow us for the remainder of our days. The police, after three years of surveillance of our persons and property, have abandoned that endeavor. But we are cautious and mistrusting of all law enforcement officials. How sad it is for us to teach our grandchild not to trust anyone, especially the police.

I believe in my heart that because of the efforts of Jack Goodwinson, through his intervention at the attorney general's office via his connections there, Skip Baldini has all but sabotaged his wife's desire to fill a vacancy of one of the numerous available judgeships. Skip Baldini sold his soul, and more than likely his wife's too, to the devil for a dollar. Skip Baldini knew exactly what was going on; he knew what sort of a person Stefan was and that he was a psychopath. However, he was so consumed with his personal vendetta against me that he perceived Stefan as a means to an end. It will be interesting to see down the road how his and his wife's lives will play out. I am a firm believer that what goes around comes around. Skip and Babs have children, and there is evil all around them.

Melinda has endured the humiliation, embarrassment, and degradation of serving more than two hundred days in prison for having committed not a single crime. And she endured following rigorous rules and regulations that were meant to control people who had criminal intent or had become hardened criminals when she entered the prison system. She endured serving time with women whose children she was responsible for removing from their homes and who threatened her bodily harm each and every day. They often complained to prison officials that Melinda had done something contrary to the rules. The infractions added punitive sanctions to her minimal privileges. She endured not seeing her son for most of this time, especially knowing that Stefan had been given sole custody.

She worked at menial jobs, picking up trash along the highway or cleaning the grounds at the prison. She endured, every day, the possibility of being dragged into court in handcuffs and shackles and paraded in front of her husband and his family and girlfriends for their amusement and enjoyment, like she was a piece of rubbish. She endured the rancid food in an amount barely adequate to keep her alive. She endured the strip searches after each and every visit and whenever a correctional officer thought it necessary. It was paramount for her on a daily basis to try to figure out how to keep herself safe for that day. Life was a day-to-day existence, and it was a crapshoot at best.

Being a parent is to love unconditionally. Being Melinda's mother is awe inspiring in the way she has held her head high and conducted herself in a brave and courageous demeanor while at all times keeping her son first and foremost.

I was emboldened by her fearless determination to persevere when all trust had been betrayed. Her confidence and poise helped me to keep my best foot moving forward. It helped me to reach out to others when I believed we were alone or abandoned by all and know that we were not in fact alone. There is a multitude of people out there who have been the victims of spousal abuse and domestic violence. They've had their children taken from them and custody given to the opposing parent, who is a sociopath or sexually or emotionally abusive. Tragically, we are not alone.

It has become incumbent upon me to serve as a spokesperson before the legislators of our state to change our laws. We need to show some mercy in aiding the expunging of criminal records for someone, such as Melinda, who has been the victim of extenuating circumstances leading to a manufactured arrest record. We need to change the laws presently on the books surrounding probation laws that immediately incarcerate anyone on probation for a violation of that probation simply because someone has the ability to manipulate the criminal justice system to further their own circumstances. Our laws are fundamentally unfair. Our laws, as they exist, leave the doors wide open for unbridled abuse of the system and serve further to re-victimize victims of domestic violence.

Many things in life are not as they seem. And unless someone takes the time to bring them to the fore, the true meaning would remain forever hidden, just as they do in the judicial system. We need to bring wrongs out into the open and develop our laws based on the injustices being perpetrated on an unknowing society.

No one expects that they are going to become a victim of a sociopath or a person with a psychopathic personality. No one ever plans for that. But the sad reality is that these people are all around us, and it does no one any good to discover this after the fact.

No one in our family wishes any malice toward Stefan or anyone in his family. It is not for us to judge them. We are strong in our beliefs that they, as well as we, will all be judged by the ultimate of judges on that final day.